C0-AUQ-706

IN PURSUIT OF PEACE

ISSUES AND SPOKESMEN SERIES

A RANDOM HOUSE STUDY IN SPEECH

GENERAL EDITOR | Don Geiger | *University of California, Berkeley*

IN PURSUIT OF PEACE

Speeches of the Sixties

edited by
DONALD W. ZACHARIAS
The University of Texas

Random House
NEW YORK

Library of Congress Catalog Card Number: 74-109112
Manufactured in the United States of America

FIRST EDITION
9 8 7 6 5 4 3 2 1

For Alan
and Eric

PREFACE

The *Issues and Spokesmen Series* has been developed as a response to a need widely expressed in the areas of rhetoric and public address: in public speaking and written composition, in speech fundamentals, discussion, argumentation, and persuasion, and in rhetorical, political, and social criticism. Broadly, instructors and students of these matters desire an enriched rhetorical substance to complement the prevailing emphasis on method and general principles.

What is particularly needed, we agree in department meetings and at conventions, are more collections of speeches and writings focused on a significant theme or problem; or we search for concrete models of excellent persuasion and argument in connection with questions truly relevant to our students' increasingly active interest in "participatory" democracy; or we want materials that will encourage depth and range in critical analysis of particular problems, as we also wish for more studies designed to excite students to independent research; or we seek striking illustrations of the ways in which speakers and writers strive to effect politically and socially consequential attitudes and decisions. These are the kinds of material that the Random House series of books on *Issues and Spokesmen* will help to supply.

Certainly I do not suggest that these books will exhaust our educational need for speeches and writings that mean business in the realm of public affairs, or that they are our only available resources. My more sober aim, having identified the *Issues and Spokesmen* books as essays in provisioning rhetoric with appropriate substance, is to describe briefly the general design and pattern of this group of books.

The term "Issues" in the series title is best understood in the popular sense of "matter the decision of which is of special or public importance," and each book focuses on a significant controversy or question of public policy. Thus each volume contains a selection by its author-editor of speeches, or speeches and writings, by important spokesmen organized around an issue of major contemporary importance or importance to its time and clear relevance to our own. Each book also contains its author-editor's fairly long essay, covering all or some of such matters as the social, political, and intellectual environment of the issue; the background of the issue in history and rhetorical tradition; a description of the careers and roles of the spokesmen involved; or an account of the rhetorical techniques and the principles of analysis with which the student will be concerned as he becomes familiar with the issue and re-examines the speeches and writings. Speeches are presented chronologically and, wherever possible, in their entirety.

Headnotes and footnotes serve familiar functions—identifying speakers, the immediate occasion of a given speech, allusions requiring explanation, and the like. In addition, special interrogative footnotes draw the student more thoughtfully into the speech—its language, line of argument, and techniques. Questions and comments in these footnotes are not intended to preempt the student's own critical focus. Rather, they will serve as suggestive examples of what perceptive critics notice and question when analyzing a test. Broader implications of the speeches and writings are considered in each volume's section for inquiry and bibliography. The latter material serves as an inductive guide to students' further examination and discussion of a given issue.

Since my purpose is to comment generally, I shall say little about that which is nonetheless the most important aspect of the series, the individuality of the separate works. Each of these books bears the distinctive stamp of its editor or coeditors; and each book represents an independent interest in substance and approach, as in toto the volumes reflect the common interests of expert students of the rhetoric of public affairs. I think that many other readers will share my admiration for the workmanship of the individual authors of these volumes and take pleasure in their educational contributions.

Don Geiger

CONTENTS

IN PURSUIT OF PEACE

Introduction

Can War Be Eliminated?

The threat of nuclear or biological war remains one of the greatest hazards for all men. However, the probability that the universe will end as "thin uniform soup"[1] decreased in the 1960s. The era began with optimism about conquering new frontiers and saw American public opinion give its blessings to a Peace Corps, a partial nuclear test-ban treaty, and increased discussion about disarmament. But it also endured crises in Berlin and Cuba; witnessed the assassinations of a president, a peace candidate for the presidential nomination, and a Nobel Peace Prize winner; and ended, despite the Paris talks, with violence still raging in Southeast Asia. Although most thoughtful policy makers reject Carl von Clausewitz's classic dictum that war is a continuation of politics by other means, the waging of war and the preparation for far greater wars continue.

The extent of this preparation is best described by scientist Linus Pauling: "If tomorrow there were to be a war, in one day, equivalent in explosive energy to the whole six years of the Second World War, and the following day another, and so on, day after day, then in 52,000 days, 146 years, the stockpiles of nuclear weapons would be exhausted."[2] In addition, the

[1] Kenneth Boulding, *The Image* (Ann Arbor, Mich.: The University of Michigan Press, 1956), p. 19.

[2] Linus Pauling, "Peace on Earth: The Position of the Scientists," *Bulletin of the Atomic Scientists*, XXIII (October 1967), 47. Dr. Ralph Lapp estimates the United States' stockpile of nuclear weapons is equivalent to about 50,000 of the bombs that fell on Hiroshima (*The New York Times*, December 29, 1968).

major powers of the world are reportedly spending $500 million annually to develop deadly botulinus toxin, yellow-fever virus, or anthrax spore that would kill hundreds of millions of people inexpensively.[3]

These are the circumstances under which Americans must live and work. For a citizen who wants to participate in the search for peace, the issues requiring his judgment are far too numerous and complex to be treated in one volume. Nevertheless, by reexamining the speeches of scientific, political, religious, and military leaders of this decade, he can better determine which issues are important, which stands on them are possible or reasonable, and which arguments for each of these stands are significant.

Besides revealing the hopes and dreams of spokesmen capable of influencing the destiny of Americans, these speeches exemplify numerous rhetorical situations. They offer the student of speech primary material from which to discover and evaluate rhetorical strategies.

Without exception, each speaker is concerned about future hazards to peace. While there are sharp differences on how to pursue peace, there is no disagreement concerning its desirability. Hopefully, concentrated study of these ten speeches will improve the dialogue between policy makers and the worried men and women who, now or in the future, carry the burden of building a world without war.

Before proceeding, it is necessary to define *peace*. Like many concepts, it is tossed around freely and allowed to mean whatever the speaker or writer wishes. In the semantic jungle of peace, the Strategic Air Command soothes the consciences of its nuclear bomber crews by giving them the motto, "Peace Is Our Profession." Equally as inventive, the Soviet government uses peace to mean primarily "an invitation to non-Communists never to resist Soviet aggression."[4]

[3] Pauling, "Peace on Earth," p. 47. See also Walter Schneir, "The Campaign To Make Chemical Warfare Respectable," *The Reporter,* XXI (October 1, 1959), 24–28.

[4] Stefan T. Possony, *Wordmanship: Semantics as a Communist Weapon* (Washington, D.C.: U.S. Government Printing Office, 1961), p. 10.

In his American University speech President Kennedy called peace "a process—a way of solving problems" and thought it based "on a series of concrete actions and effective agreements which are in the interests of all concerned." (See pp. 60–70.) Arthur I. Waskow, noted analyst of domestic and international conflicts, considers peace "a situation in which war—organized violence between nations—is extremely unlikely or impossible, and in which the values and liberties that Americans cherish are being protected and advanced."[5] In his monumental study of war, Quincy Wright, a recipient of numerous awards for his research in international relations, defines peace generally as "an equilibrium among many forces," and specifically as "the condition of a community in which order and justice prevail, internally among its members and externally in its relations with other communities."[6] It is Wright's definition that best describes the use of peace in this study. It means not merely an absence of war or a Pax Americana, but a complex condition characterized by order and justice.

Peace, of course, does not mean an absence of conflict between nations or within a nation, but it does require an absence of armed conflict and a predisposition on the part of disputants to resolve their differences through diplomacy or adjudication. All nations must find it mutually beneficial to use international agencies, which are yet to be designed and created, for the resolution of conflicts or the advocacy of social, economic, and political changes. Debates over which agencies are to be created, what powers are to be granted them, and how national sovereignty is to be preserved are still raging. In short, a concept of international justice is still being evolved. This concept is an important one because whatever genuine peace the world enjoys will be in direct proportion to the quality of international justice.

Equally as important as a definition of peace is the ques-

[5] Arthur I. Waskow, *The Worried Man's Guide to World Peace* (Garden City, N.Y.: Anchor Books, 1963), p. xv.

[6] Quincy Wright, *A Study of War,* 2nd ed. (Chicago: The University of Chicago Press, 1965), pp. 864 and 1284.

tion, "Can war be eliminated?" An examination of nature reveals a curious phenomenon—only ants and men practice the art of war. Ants, according to entomologists, are doomed to continue their warring ways. Fortunately, anthropologists and biologists are not so sure about men. Margaret Mead suggests that "we belong to the first generation that has actually had a chance to consider the prevention of war because for the first time in history modern forms of warfare, particularly nuclear warfare, make warfare catastrophic for *all* of those who engage in it."[7] Her belief in man's ability to survive is predicated on his power to muster political support for institutions designed to prevent war.

Meanwhile, a debate concerning whether or not man is born with aggressive instincts continues among psychologists. At this point one conclusion seems sure: these drives do not account for war. An individual, however pugnacious or frustrated, "lacks the capacity to make organized warfare."[8] His drives, nevertheless, do originate behavior patterns that in turn create the psychological climate appropriate for making war. But the ultimate decision to commit a nation to war is a leadership function and not the outgrowth of individual or mass emotion.

In short, there is no evidence to show that man has suddenly shed his aggressive behavior and become a pacific creature. Even though nations have been unable to avoid limited wars in recent years, there is some comfort in realizing that no country has used a nuclear bomb on another since 1945. What will happen in the future, of course, depends on numerous people and events: Soviet policy, the belligerency of Communist China, the political development of Africa, and the acquisition of nuclear weapons by additional countries. Also destined to play a key role in determining the inevitability of

[7] Quoted in Christoph von Furer-Haimendorf, "Violence: Can We Break the Habit?" *Saturday Review,* LI (June 1, 1968), 28.

[8] Alastair Buchan, *War in Modern Society* (London: C. A. Watts, 1966), p. 4. See also Morton Deutsch, "A Psychological Basis for Peace," in *Preventing World War III,* eds. Quincy Wright, William M. Evan, and Morton Deutsch (New York: Simon and Schuster, 1962), p. 371.

war are those who shape American foreign policy and who must win popular support for their policies. Will they, for instance, continue to exhort the electorate by using fear appeals and stressing the negative aspects of disarmament? What arguments and incentives can spokesmen for peace offer which will make preparation for peace as popular as preparation for war? What role should speechmaking play in shaping public opinion on this issue? One way to begin the search for answers to these questions and understand the problem of achieving peace is to study key speeches of the sixties.

To understand the speeches on peace we need to look critically at language. Modern rhetoricians have frequently noted the bipolarity of English and the difficulties this presents for the national leader who chooses the role of conciliator. Nowhere is this condition more evident than in the speeches of war and peace. Policies are considered capable of bringing only "victory" or "defeat" to the West. Our weapons are "defensive," but our enemy's weapons are always "offensive." Military forces are judged according to their "preparedness" or "unpreparedness." The major countries in the world must be either "armed" or "disarmed." Perhaps the most revealing bipolar division is the tendency to speak only of "communist" and "noncommunist" countries.

A study of the metaphors used to promote peace is even more revealing, for it shows how easily our thinking becomes stereotyped and how the actual condition we are trying to describe is forgotten. "Missile gap," for example, was a popular figure in the election of 1960. The public is reminded regularly that the United States and Russia are engaged in an "arms race." Finding this concept misleading, Max Lerner has recommended that it be replaced with "deadly spiral."[9] Other time-worn metaphors are "nuclear deterrence" and "one world." Undoubtedly, the most overworked of all is the post–World War II term "cold war."

Debates in the 1960s were filled with references to "clean weapons," "fail safe," "fire storm," "overkill," "megacorpses,"

[9] Max Lerner, *The Age of Overkill* (New York: Simon and Schuster, 1962), p. 34.

"nuclear pacifist," "fallout shelter," "broken arrows," "commitment," and "escalation." The nuclear vocabulary, in fact, has expanded so rapidly that Donald M. Kaplan and Armand Schwerner have compiled a *Domesday Dictionary* to help the novice.[10]

This focus on the language of the speeches is not intended to imply that a removal of all semantic problems would dissolve the differences among policy makers or between Americans and Russians. It does show, however, one of the major rhetorical problems confronting a spokesman for peace: the circumstances are already complex enough without letting clichés or stereotypes trigger hostilities or cause greater misunderstandings.[11]

Scientists on Peace

The chief scientific inheritance of the 1960s was the technology for producing and stockpiling nuclear and thermonuclear weapons. If the men who helped develop these weapons agreed upon their destructiveness and the best systems for protecting innocent victims from their use, private citizens and statesmen could make policy decisions with greater ease. However, like most professionals, scientists do not always concur when matters of science and politics meet.

Albert Einstein, for example, spent the final working hours of his life drafting a speech to be delivered over a television and radio network in celebration of Israel's Independence Day in 1955. He characterized the conflict between East and West as "an old-style struggle for power," but a conflict with a new twist. "The difference," he said, "is that, this time, the development of atomic power has imbued the struggle with a

[10] New York: Simon and Schuster, 1963.

[11] For further study of language problems, see Anatol Rapoport, "Rules for Debate," in *Preventing World War III* (New York, 1962), pp. 246–262; Edmund S. Glenn, "Semantic Difficulties in International Communication," in *The Use and Misuse of Language,* ed. S. I. Hayakawa (Greenwich, Conn.: Fawcett Publications, 1962), pp. 47–69; and W. Phillips Davison, *International Political Communication* (New York: Frederick A. Praeger, 1965).

ghostly character; for both parties know and admit that, should the quarrel deteriorate into actual war, mankind is doomed."[12]

Although most scientists share Einstein's belief on the outcome of war, they disagree markedly on how to avoid a nuclear confrontation. Certainly many of them would not accept his pronouncement that an "armaments race is the *worst* possible method of preventing an open conflict" and that "real peace cannot be reached without systematic disarmament on a supranational scale."[13] What, then, are the views of American scientists? How great is their influence on government policy? How do they use speeches to exert their influence?

Scientists who have openly taken positions on questions of peace can be divided into three groups. The first includes men who, like Edward Teller, believe that the "best guarantee of peace is appropriate force in the hands of those who want peace."[14] Teller's position clearly reflects the moral dilemmas of modern scientists who recognize peace as the question of overriding importance. For them, peace can be maintained only by preparing for war. Military preparedness and continued development of new weapons are more reliable than agreements with the Soviets. Hastily concluded treaties may lead to a weakening of America's defenses. Consequently, Teller became the most prominent scientist to speak against the nuclear test-ban treaty. In his testimony before the Senate Preparedness Investigating Subcommittee, he told the members that ratification of the treaty would have "grave consequences for the security of the United States" and the security of the free world.[15] A few weeks later he appeared on "Meet the Press" and again denounced the treaty. "It is our

[12] Otto Nathan and Heinz Norden, eds., *Einstein on Peace* (New York: Simon and Schuster, 1960), p. 640.

[13] *Ibid.*, p. 528.

[14] Edward Teller, "BMD in a Strategy for Peace," in *Arms Control for the Late Sixties,* eds. James E. Dougherty and J. F Lehman, Jr. (Princeton, N J.: D. Van Nostrand Company, 1967), p. 117.

[15] Edward Teller, *Congressional Record,* 88th Cong., 1st Sess. (August 20, 1963), p. 15489.

strength," Teller said, "that is preserving the peace in our dangerous world."[16]

America's most gifted advocate of nuclear deterrence—sometimes called the balance-of-terror policy—is Herman Kahn, a physicist and director of the Hudson Institute, a "think factory" for devising defense strategy. In 1959 Kahn gave a series of lectures at the Princeton University Center of International Studies and later published them as *On Thermonuclear War*.[17]

His book became the most controversial scientific work of the year and left its imprint upon defense policy. After exploring the possibility and even the probability of another world war, Kahn suggested that nuclear war would not spell the destruction of civilization. His analysis was frequently praised for its realistic view of war and just as frequently attacked for its "bloodthirsty irrationality." In addition to his highly influential role in determining defense strategies, Kahn has lectured extensively before private groups and at colleges and universities, including the Air War College, the University of Chicago, and Harvard and Princeton universities. His most recent contribution to the study of nuclear strategies is the technique of using metaphors and scenarios to explore the condition of a country after a nuclear attack.[18]

Located between the deterrers and the members of the peace movement are scientists like Hans Bethe and Jerome Wiesner. A part-time consultant on defense matters, Bethe has twice represented the United States as a disarmament negotiator at Geneva. He advocates minimum deterrence, "perhaps two hundred missiles and bombers on each side, carefully controlled by treaty."[19] Wiesner, President Kennedy's science adviser from 1960 to 1963, takes a similar view. He opposed

[16] *Ibid.*, p. 17044 (September 16, 1963).

[17] Princeton, N.J.: Princeton University Press, 1960. See also his *Thinking About the Unthinkable* (New York: Horizon Press, 1962).

[18] See Herman Kahn, *On Escalation: Metaphors and Scenarios* (New York: Frederick A. Praeger, 1965).

[19] See Arthur Herzog, *The War-Peace Establishment* (New York: Harper and Row, 1965), p. 148.

the increase in United States missile forces under the Kennedy administration and called for 200 relatively secure missiles for deterrence. Together with Herbert F. York, Wiesner has argued that a sound antimissile defense system cannot be developed. "Both sides in the arms race," they conclude, "are thus confronted by the dilemma of steadily increasing military power and steadily decreasing national security. *It is our considered professional judgment that this dilemma has no technical solution."*[20] The solution that remains is, of course, a political one reached through major disarmament agreements.

The third position taken by scientists on the question of nuclear war is active participation in peace organizations whose aims are the elimination of war as a system for resolving international disputes. The champion of this point of view is Linus Pauling, winner of two Nobel prizes and author of *No More War!* Formerly a professor of chemistry at the California Institute of Technology at Pasadena, Pauling is currently on the staff of the Center for the Study of Democratic Institutions. His campaign for peace has taken him on speaking tours in the United States, where he addresses approximately 25,000 people each year, and, in 1963, on a lecture tour of South America. He hopes ultimately to see the abolition of war, but his more immediate goals are to stop the testing of all nuclear weapons and to establish the World Peace Research Organization.[21]

In his speech to the American Association for the Advancement of Science in 1961, British novelist C. P. Snow called scientists the most important occupational group in the world today. "At this moment," he said, "what they do is of passionate concern to the whole of human society." (See pp. 32–45.) Their views on the best route to peace have to be considered carefully. Much of their research is federally financed and directly or indirectly related to national defense.

[20] Jerome Wiesner and Herbert F. York, "National Security and the Nuclear Test-Ban," *Scientific American*, CCXI (October 1964), 32–35.

[21] Linus Pauling, *No More War!* (New York: Dodd, Mead and Company, 1958), pp. 11–12.

Their influence on political questions was confirmed again in 1967 by the announcement that thirty-five of the nation's most distinguished scientists and scholars had acted secretly as advisers on military problems in Vietnam.[22]

The dialogue between scientists and the public improved in the 1960s. The individual scientists listed here, and numerous others like them, have spoken at professional meetings, lectured at colleges and universities, and talked to student and adult groups. In further recognition of their responsibilities they have formed new groups to disseminate scientific information. Scientific experts supplied by the Federation of American Scientists have regularly addressed community groups on the problems of nuclear weapons and disarmament. The Scientists' Committee for Radiation Information in New York and the Committee on Nuclear Information in St. Louis have supplied information on many questions pertaining to nuclear attack and civil defense. If they can be judged by their speeches and their publications, scientists in America have accepted the moral un-neutrality of science and the necessity of participating in politics.

Politics of Arms Control

When John F. Kennedy took office in January 1961, he became commander in chief of the world's largest arsenal of nuclear weapons. He also inherited a defense policy based chiefly upon the doctrine of massive nuclear retaliation. While this strategy was generally conceded to have inhibited nuclear war, it did not eliminate the danger of accidental war or prevent limited war, fought with non-nuclear weapons. Furthermore, limited wars carry with them the danger of escalating into nuclear wars. Thus President Kennedy and the American people faced some fundamental questions at the beginning of the 1960s: (1) Had war become obsolete as an instrument of national policy? (2) Had war become ineffective as an instrument of defense? (3) Had the balance of power system lost its effectiveness as a means of providing

[22] Louisville *Courier-Journal*, December 29, 1967.

world stability? (4) Could transition from a tradition of power politics to one of international law and organization be made suddenly or only gradually?[23] These issues were grossly oversimplified in the question of the era: "Is it better to be Red than dead?" Most Americans believed it was possible to be neither one nor the other.

An examination of one political decision made by the United States in concert with the Soviet Union and Great Britain in 1963 provides some insights into its position on these major issues. At the beginning of the decade, disarmament talks had been conducted at Geneva for fifteen years without any accomplishments save a short moratorium on nuclear testing in the atmosphere. On September 1, 1961, during the Berlin crisis, the Soviets broke the agreement and resumed testing. In February 1962, the United States resumed its atmospheric tests. By March, however, both countries agreed to renew the test-ban negotiations at Geneva. After President Kennedy's American University address on June 10, 1963, negotiators from the United States, Great Britain, and Russia met in Moscow to draw up a partial nuclear test-ban treaty. By the end of the year most nations, with the notable exceptions of France and Communist China, had ratified the treaty barring nuclear-weapons tests in the atmosphere, outer space, and under water.

During this same period the major powers survived the Berlin crisis (1961), and the Cuban crises (1961 and 1962), without turning to the use of nuclear weapons. Despite reports of ten nuclear accidents (called "broken arrows" in the Defense Department) by the United States alone, none caused nuclear explosions. Not included in this total is the famous 1966 incident at Palomares, Spain, involving the crash of a B–52 SAC plane carrying four hydrogen bombs. One technical report on accidental explosions estimated the chances in the 1960s were one to a hundred that a United States nuclear weapon would explode at some time in the next ten years. The report closed with a somber note: "The extremely approximate estimate is for essentially mechanical malfunctions

[23] See Wright, *A Study of War,* p. 1521.

only: we make no attempt to quantify the various possibilities of human error."[24] These are just a few of the political and mechanical problems interfering with prevention of World War III.

Under these circumstances the 1960s witnessed renewed interest in disarmament, or what most government leaders preferred to call "arms control." At the beginning of the decade the Soviet Union and the United States offered plans for general and complete disarmament. President Kennedy, for example, in his 1961 speech to the UN General Assembly, outlined the United States' approach and called for the development of international peace-keeping machinery to control the reduction in national forces, to inspect the disarming countries, and to enforce the disarmament arrangements. Unfortunately, Premier Nikita Khrushchev's counterproposal rejected the idea of international supervision and the plan died.

In the years since ratification of the partial test-ban treaty, the United States and the Soviet Union have shifted from discussion of complete disarmament to questions of arms control. The new issues are the effect of arms control on the Atlantic alliance, the future of Germany, ballistic missile defense, the proliferation of nuclear weapons, and limited wars. In effect, arms control is a more permissive term because it accepts the continued existence of national military establishments. Although the merits of continuing negotiations with the Soviet Union have often been challenged, they have led the world back a few steps from a nuclear abyss.

Despite this search for peace through arms control, several important questions remain unanswered: If there were mutual intent to keep an agreement, would complete disarmament make for a more stable world? Do military forces play an essential role in preserving peace? If the military power of the major nations were eliminated, would local wars flare up in Latin America, the Middle East, or elsewhere?[25]

[24] John B. Phelps, *et al.*, *Accidental War: Some Dangers in the 1960's* quoted in *Congressional Record,* 86th Cong., 2nd Sess. (August 12, 1960), p. 16268.

[25] Jerome H. Spingarn, *New Approaches to Arms Control* (New York: Foreign Policy Association—World Affairs Center, 1962), p. 40.

Senator Barry Goldwater and the Republican party of 1964 had answers. Throughout his campaign for the Presidency, Goldwater reminded Americans that communism was a global threat. "Only if we keep our eyes open and guard up," he warned, "can we prevent war."[26] Indeed, Goldwater's constant attack upon the military policies of the Kennedy-Johnson administration and his proposal to give tactical commanders in the field more "leeway" to respond to an enemy with nuclear weapons earned him the sobriquet "trigger-happy." Even though he insisted that he was "preoccupied with peace," he could never clarify the ambiguity in his call for the United States to use its "great national power" to keep peace from slipping away.

Over four months before he received his party's nomination, Goldwater gave a preview of his campaign strategy in a Detroit speech, unleashing a devastating attack upon Secretary of Defense Robert McNamara. (See pp. 73–83.) McNamara, rather than President Johnson, remained the target for his most bitter pronouncements on American defense policy. In a speech to the American Legion National Convention he condemned the "let's be friends" attitude toward the Soviet Union and accused McNamara of trying to turn the Defense Department into a "Disarmament Department." "Appease an aggressor and try to make friends with him," he told members of the Legion, "and eventually you'll have to go to war with him."[27] If any doubt about his position on disarmament and communism remained, he clarified it in this speech: "Now, if we want to halt their gains, if we want to save America's future and freedom, we must be stronger than the enemy—not just by a little bit, but by far."[28]

Neither the Kennedy-Johnson administration nor the election of 1964 answered the questions stated at the beginning of this unit. But public acceptance of the test-ban treaty and the overwhelming defeat of Goldwater indicated a popular weari-

[26] Barry Goldwater, "Acceptance Speech," *Vital Speeches of the Day,* XXX (August 15, 1964), 642.

[27] Barry Goldwater, "The Will To Be Strong," *Vital Speeches of the Day,* XXXI (October 15, 1964), 7.

[28] *Ibid.,* p. 5.

ness of "big stick" policies toward America's enemies. Hidden, perhaps, in the results of the election was the message to President Johnson that Americans were tired of playing a nuclear version of Russian roulette. By the mid-1960s the public mood called for gradual arms control, not more arms.

Religion and War

Every generation has believed that its war was a just defense of values that could not otherwise be protected and that its war would be the last. When their nation goes to war, churchmen have traditionally interpreted this action from one of three points of view: a crusade, pacificism, or a just war. Though a few may advocate a crusading war against atheists, this doctrine is so alien to the question of peace that it does not merit treatment here. Some ministers, of course, would like to side-step the whole issue of war and peace and do what they call "preaching of the gospel." C. Wright Mills addressed his famous "Pagan Sermon to the Christian Clergy" to these ministers. After charging that religion had become a dependent variable in social and personal matters, he asked, ". . . who among you is considering what it means for Christians to kill men and women and children in ever more efficient and impersonal ways?"[29]

The Mennonites, the Church of the Brethren, Jehovah's Witnesses, and the Society of Friends (Quakers) have assumed a pacifist position throughout their histories, although not all members of these groups are pacifists. The American Friends Service Committee, for instance, consists of Quakers actively committed to the creation of nonviolent methods of solving disputes. "Pacifism," according to Charles E. Pickett of the AFSC, "is a way of life that you apply to all areas of life." A pacifist is expected to bear witness, which means to Pickett: "standing up for one's conscience with the purpose of influencing others."[30] But pacifists disagree on goals. Some, like W. H. Ferry and Mulford Sibley, advocate unilateral disarma-

[29] *Nation,* CLXXXVI (March 8, 1958), 202.

[30] Herzog, *The War-Peace Establishment,* pp. 232 and 233.

ment. Others, like Pickett, urge pacifists to take an active role in picketing Soviet embassies and in similar actions to compel the Soviets to disarm too.

Regardless of their division on issues, pacifists usually look to the late A. J. Muste, an ordained Presbyterian minister, for ideological guidance. In explaining his commitment to peace he said, "My own mainspring . . . is my religious faith."[31] Based chiefly upon religious and moral convictions, pacifism holds that violence is intrinsically immoral and should not be condoned, regardless of the circumstances. In stating the classic doctrine of pacifism for the 1960s Muste declared, "Nonconformity, Holy Disobedience, becomes a virtue, indeed a necessary and indispensable measure of spiritual self-preservation, in a day when the impulse to conform, to acquiesce, . . . is used as an instrument to subject men to totalitarian rule and involve them in permanent war."[32]

Pacifism has always been a belief held by a minority of Americans and has had only limited influence upon foreign policy. In fact, one pacifist has suggested that if peace is preserved it will be through the efforts of "peace-minded nonpacifists, who do not renounce war absolutely, but who oppose war in our time on grounds of the humanitarian and pragmatic."[33]

More than any others in this decade, two events rekindled among church leaders an interest in the morality of war. The first is Pope John XXIII's *Pacem in Terris* encyclical of April 9, 1963—the first ever addressed not only to Catholics but "to all men of goodwill." It is virtually impossible to overemphasize the impact of the Pope's statement that "Justice, . . . right reason and humanity urgently demand that the arms race should cease" and that future disputes should be settled by negotiations.[34] Rhetoricians have yet to determine the

[31] *Ibid.*, p. 245.

[32] Nat Hentoff, ed., *The Essays of A. J. Muste* (Indianapolis: Bobbs-Merrill, 1967), p. 372.

[33] Roland H. Bainton, *Christian Attitudes Towards War and Peace* (Nashville, Tenn.: Abingdon Press, 1960), p. 253.

[34] A copy of the encyclical is reprinted in *The New York Times*, April 11, 1963.

value of this document as a source or arguments for American clergymen of all faiths. But even a casual examination of sermons, magazine articles, and books written after the encyclical shows its influence.

The second event to influence church leaders was the escalation of the Vietnam conflict. Questions pertaining to the ethics of force in the nuclear age now concern draft-age teenagers and their parents as well as theologians who have struggled with this issue since 1945. The complexity of the fighting in Vietnam does not permit an easy application of the "just-war" theory. This theory is usually advocated most successfully when an enemy can be cast in the satanic role of working to destroy all that is virtuous, just, and godly in the world. Nations which oppose this demonic force claim for themselves the task of executing God's will and the further virtue of annihilating or routing the enemy humanely. In America's first televised war, the pictures of villages being destroyed and noncombatants being burned by napalm arouse cries of moral anguish. No one considers the enemy's tactics any less repugnant, but the margin of justice claimed by Americans and South Vietnamese leaders is too narrow.

Jewish, Catholic, and Protestant clergymen throughout the United States have examined the morality of America's policy. Their actions deserve a more detailed study, but the collection of sermons delivered in 1967 and published as *The Vietnam War: Christian Perspectives*[35] offers a good survey of the movement. One address in particular stands out above the others. Delivered in New York City at a meeting sponsored by Clergy and Laymen Concerned about Vietnam, Dr. Martin Luther King, Jr.'s sermon mirrors the sentiments of many who oppose the war: "Somehow this madness must cease. I speak as a child of God and brother to the suffering poor of Vietnam and the poor of America who are paying the double price of smashed hopes at home and death and corruption in Vietnam."[36]

[35] Edited by Michael P. Hamilton (Grand Rapids, Mich.: William B. Eerdmans Publishing Co., 1967).

[36] *Ibid.*, p. 123.

Not all clergymen oppose the war in Vietnam, and most believe that military power is a necessary ingredient of national power. Events of the 1960s, however, revived the debate about the morality of war and caused more clergymen and laymen to become active spokesmen for peace.

Military Establishment and Peace

Shortly before he left office, President Eisenhower warned Americans of the military-industrial complex's growing influence on government. In a 1963 speech, Secretary of Defense McNamara pointed out that his department spent 10 percent of the national income, directly or indirectly employed 3.7 million people, and absorbed over half of every tax dollar. Under these circumstances, the political and economic power of the Pentagon has to be considered when discussing peace.

The basic purpose of the military, according to a 1962 Senate subcommittee report, is "to be prepared for war and to fight and win if war should come."[37] In the United States the military exists only to enforce national policy. But numerous questions related to this doctrine were raised at the beginning of the Kennedy administration after Secretary McNamara issued a directive stating that defense officials should "avoid discussion of foreign policy matters."[38] Feeling that their speeches had been unduly muzzled, numerous military officials sent complaints to the Senate Committee on Armed Services. The Committee immediately launched a full-scale investigation of the use of military personnel and facilities to arouse public sentiment toward the cold war and to indoctrinate men in the armed services.

After conducting hearings and collecting over 3,000 pages of testimony, a subcommittee reconfirmed the principle of civilian control of the military through the executive branch and recommended that military personnel not "engage or partici-

[37] Report by the Special Preparedness Subcommittee of the Committee on Armed Services, *Military Cold War Education and Speech Review Policies,* 87th Cong., 2nd Sess., p. 2.

[38] *Ibid.*, p. 17.

pate" in politics. While the subcommittee strongly advised that military opinion be sought during the development of defense policies, at the same time it supported the right of the Defense Department to control criticism of administration policy by reviewing and censoring public speeches of military personnel. Officers who found administration policy unacceptable were advised to resign and join the ranks of other dissenters.[39]

Although this report covered a segment of civilian and military relations that could cause civilian authorities much public embarrassment, it did not directly face the question of how much power was held by the military in shaping policy. Without question, the Joint Chiefs of Staff, headed by General Earle Wheeler, comprise the most important military board in history. Supported by a staff of 1,800 officers, enlisted men, and civilians, they work together primarily to funnel competent military information to the President and to translate national policy into military action. In addition to these major responsibilities, General Wheeler has assumed a key role in winning public support for the administration's Vietnam policy by making speeches throughout the country. (See pp. 132–139.) [40]

General Wheeler has been assisted in this undertaking by others, the most notable being General William Westmoreland, former commander of American troops in Vietnam. General Westmoreland's trip from Vietnam to address Congress in April 1967, can hardly be described as a military mission. Public reaction to his speech clearly showed the attention that a military figure can command in the American political forum.[41]

Not all generals, of course, endorse the views of the administration under which they serve. After they resign or retire, they often feel a compulsion to harangue the public, write a

[39] *Ibid.*, pp. 3–6.

[40] See Earle Wheeler, "Vietnam: A Military Appraisal," *Vital Speeches of the Day*, XXXIV (August 1, 1968), 613–615.

[41] The text of his speech to Congress is in *The New York Times*, April 29, 1967.

book, and bombard senators with suggestions. In many ways this is an apt description of Lieutenant General James M. Gavin, who resigned from the army in 1958 because he opposed the Defense Department's policy of de-emphasizing conventional arms development. After 1966, his former status as a general was used by those who opposed President Johnson's Vietnam policy. In hearings of the Senate Committee on Foreign Relations he was asked specifically to give an appraisal of United States military strategy in Vietnam. (See pp. 118–128.)[42] His comments were no less political than General Westmoreland's.

Some would argue that the Vietnam conflict has brought with it "a huge military machine which cannot be fully understood or managed by the few civilian politicians who temporarily hold the reins of office."[43] Others reject the idea of any erosion of civilian control but caution that when policy decisions are made, numerous pressure groups are at work, including the military ones. The increased number of speeches by leading military officials in the late 1960s indicated they were being given greater freedom to express their views, especially in support of administration policy.

Any systematic undertaking for achieving peace has to propose a plan for converting the huge defense industry into production of peacetime goods. Recognition of a military-industrial complex does not mean it is a sinister cabal. In fact, its work is usually done in the open with enthusiastic support from Congress and the American people. The complex is so deeply rooted in the American economy that in twelve states defense payrolls constitute from 10 to 30 percent of all employment in manufacturing plants.[44] An investigation conducted by one congressman disclosed that the one hundred

[42] For a transcript of the hearings, see *The Vietnam Hearings* (New York: Random House, 1966).

[43] John M. Swomley, Jr., *The Military Establishment* (Boston: Beacon Press, 1964), p. ix.

[44] Julius Duscha, "Arms and the Big Money Men," *Harper's Magazine*, CCXXVIII (March 1964), 40. The states are Arizona, California, Colorado, Connecticut, Florida, Kansas, Maryland, Missouri, New Mexico, Texas, Utah, and Washington.

biggest defense contractors had on their payrolls more than 1,400 retired officers with the rank of major or higher. Since the roster included 261 generals and admirals, it becomes fairly obvious that to have an influential military man on the industrial staff is good business.[45]

In 1963, when President Johnson advocated the decade's only proposal for a cut in military spending, the howls echoed from Washington to city courthouses around the country. With the zeal of a freshman lawmaker, Senator George McGovern recommended a cut of $5 billion in the same budget. Neither man's proposal won public support, but, over the objections of several congressmen, Secretary McNamara succeeded in closing many of the military installations. If a token cut in spending brings such cries of outrage, disarmament would undoubtedly create near panic unless a carefully prepared plan were devised for making the transition. Although it is less sinister than most questions of the nuclear age, Americans would have to ask, "Can we afford disarmament?" if an agreement were made with the Soviet Union.[46]

Vietnam: Symbol of an Era

"We will not be defeated. We will not grow tired. We will not withdraw, either openly or under the cloak of a meaningless aggreement."[47] Thus spoke President Lyndon Johnson at Johns Hopkins University, April 7, 1965, in reference to the American commitment to South Vietnam. At that time 400 Americans had lost their lives in the conflict. By September 1968, over 27,000 had been killed, an emotionally scarred nation looked for a leader who could end the war, and President Johnson had indeed grown tired.

The history of the American involvement is clearly recorded

[45] *Ibid.*, p. 47.

[46] For an analysis of this issue, see Gerard Piel, "The Economics of Disarmament," *Bulletin of Atomic Scientists,* XVI (April 1960), 117–122, 126; and Wassily W. Leontief and Marvin Hoffenberg, "The Economic Effects of Disarmament," *Scientific American,* CCIV (April 1961), 47–55.

[47] Lyndon B. Johnson, "Pattern for Peace in Southeast Asia," *Department of State Bulletin,* LII (April 26, 1965), 607–608.

in Marcus G. Raskin and Bernard B. Fall's *The Viet-Nam Reader*.[48] But what must be noted here are the actions and speeches of the dissenters which led to the President's last plea. No student of this era can ignore the resurgence of the spoken word as a basic tool for those who opposed the Johnson administration.

Early in the struggle, Secretary of Defense McNamara and General Maxwell D. Taylor predicted that the United States military task would be completed by 1965.[49] When 1965 came and there were plans to increase rather than decrease the military forces, Americans in and out of government became alarmed.

The academic community responded first to the administration's new policy and offered a preview of the resentment that was growing in the rest of the country. Faculty members, claiming a far better understanding of Asian history than the State Department, organized "teach-ins." Held first at the University of Michigan, these lecture and discussion sessions on Vietnam became the hallmark of a viable campus. More than fifty teach-ins occurred in the spring of 1965. The one national teach-in held in Washington, D.C. during May 1965, featured such prominent scholars as Ernest Nagel, B. F. Skinner, Talcott Parsons, and Hans J. Morgenthau. "The rhetoric of free expression," wrote the organizer of one teach-in, "is being translated into *action relevant to power*."[50] Unfortunately, this new strategy seemed to have little direct effect on administration policy, and it surrendered to more physical forms of protest during the summer of 1965. "The national teach-in, the Bundy debate, the International Days of Protest," one critic observed, "all seem to have been designed more to threaten non-support than to encourage productive talk."[51]

[48] New York: Random House, 1967.

[49] Marcus G. Raskin and Bernard B. Fall, *The Viet-Nam Reader* (New York: Random House, 1967), p. 129.

[50] Arnold S. Kaufman, "Teach-Ins—New Force for the Times," *Nation*, CC (June 21, 1965), 667.

[51] Howard H. Martin, "The Rhetoric of Academic Protest," *Central States Speech Journal*, XVII (November 1966), 248. See also the comments of Kenneth E. Boulding, "Reflections on Protest," *Bulletin of Atomic Scientists*, XXI (October 1965), 18–20.

Meanwhile the Senate began its probe of the administration's Vietnam policy. Some would suggest it was a result of the furor raised by the teach-ins. Senator J. William Fulbright, once a warm personal friend of President Johnson, led his colleagues Frank Church, Wayne Morse, George McGovern, Eugene McCarthy, and eventually Robert Kennedy, in challenging the new policy of escalation. When the Senate protests produced no changes, Senator Fulbright, acting as chairman of the Foreign Relations Committee, initiated the first full-scale investigation of American military policy since the hearings on President Harry Truman's firing of General Douglas MacArthur. In words that reflected the charges made against all dissenters of the day, Senator Fulbright said, "Instead of trading epithets about the legitimacy of debate, about who is and is not giving aid and comfort to the enemy, we would do well to focus calmly and deliberately on the issue itself."[52] During the next three weeks the country watched the committee on television as it examined its four key witnesses: Secretary of State Dean Rusk, Lieutenant General James M. Gavin, former ambassador George F. Kennan, and General Maxwell D. Taylor.

The hearings revealed a division in the Democratic party that President Johnson could not mend. With each escalation in troop commitments, the dissension became stronger. Finally, on November 30, 1967, Senator McCarthy announced his decision to enter the presidential primaries because of President Johnson's "evident intention to escalate and to intensify the war in Vietnam" and "the absence of any positive indication or suggestion for a compromise or for a negotiated political settlement."[53] After Senator McCarthy won the New Hampshire primary, Senator Robert Kennedy said he, too, would campaign for his party's nomination because it was "unmistakably clear that we can change these disastrous divisive policies only by changing the men who are now making them."[54] Two weeks later President Johnson succumbed to

[52] *The Vietnam Hearings,* p. xiv.

[53] *The New York Times,* December 1, 1967.

[54] *Ibid.,* March 17, 1968.

the attack upon his policies by announcing in a nationally televised speech that he would neither seek nor accept his party's nomination for another term. (See pp. 159–171.) On March 31, 1968, in an act of great personal sacrifice, President Johnson led the nation in taking a new step toward peace.

SELECTED BIBLIOGRAPHY

In addition to the sources cited in the footnotes, the following should be consulted for further reading in rhetorical criticism and the basic issues of peace.

1. Black, Edwin. *Rhetorical Criticism: A Study in Method.* New York: Macmillan, 1965. After describing the inadequacies of traditional Aristotelian studies in rhetorical criticism, Black suggests several alternatives for making criticism meaningful.
2. Claude, Inis L., Jr. *The Changing United Nations.* New York: Random House, 1967. Delivered originally as a series of lectures, this study describes the recent alterations in the basic structure of the United Nations and the conditions needed for it to play a major role in international politics.
3. Etzioni, Amitai. *The Hard Way to Peace.* New York: Crowell-Collier Press, 1962. The author argues for gradualism in disarmament as the best way for eliminating the nuclear threat since this policy promotes the reduction of international tensions, the reversal of the arms race, and an interbloc political settlement.
4. Finn, James. *Protest: Pacifism and Politics.* New York: Random House, 1968. Finn reports his interviews with leading protestors against the Vietnam war including prominent Protestant, Catholic, and Jewish churchmen, pacifists, political leaders, and conscientious objectors. He provides an excellent bibliography on the peace movement.
5. Fisher, Roger, ed. *International Conflict and Behavioral Science.* New York: Basic Books, 1964. This is a collection of essays by leading behavioral scientists who examine the role of human conduct in producing tensions between East and West.
6. Fromm, Erich. *May Man Prevail?* Garden City, N.Y.: Doubleday, 1961. Fromm describes the hazards of deterrence and argues for universal disarmament administered through the United Nations as a supernational organization.
7. Gilpin, Robert. *American Scientists and Nuclear Weapons Policy.* Princeton, N.J.: Princeton University Press, 1962. A thorough account

of the rising influence of scientists upon politics and the explanation of the intrascientific conflict over a nuclear test ban make this a fundamental work for understanding the complexities of American defense policy.

8. Griffin, Leland M. "The Rhetorical Structure of the 'New Left' Movement: Part I," *Quarterly Journal of Speech*, L (April 1964), 113–135. In an essay based upon careful examination of speeches and writings by members of the new left, Griffin outlines the development of the movement from 1949 to 1964, discusses the arguments selected to make it an active force in American politics, and assesses the effectiveness of the language and symbols used by leaders of the movement to shape American opinion on civil rights and peace.
9. Janowitz, Morris. *The Professional Soldier*. Glencoe, Ill.: Free Press, 1960. A review of the professional life, organizational setting, and leadership of the American military, this study offers an assessment of the military's power position in American society and of its behavior in international relations.
10. Kennedy, Robert F. *To Seek a Newer World*. Garden City, N.Y.: Doubleday, 1967. Based upon his work in the Senate, Kennedy comments on several issues facing America, including the ones of nuclear control, a China policy, and Vietnam.
11. Kintner, William R. *Peace and the Strategy Conflict*. New York: Frederick A. Praeger, 1967. From his research at the Foreign Policy Research Institute, Kintner argues that "the strategic nuclear superiority of the United States has been, and can continue to be, the major contribution to whatever tenuous stability the world enjoys."
12. Kissinger, Henry A., ed. *Problems of National Strategy*. New York: Frederick A. Praeger, 1965. This volume contains twenty-five essays by prominent Americans who have debated the fundamental questions pertaining to American defense policy, alliances in the nuclear age, unconventional warfare, and weapons control during the 1960s.
13. Lapp, Ralph E. *The New Priesthood*. New York: Harper and Row, 1965. A scientist and a former researcher for the famous Manhattan Project, Lapp analyzes the impact of science upon society, particularly how scientists use their recently acquired power to influence the public and politicians.
14. Melman, Seymour, ed. *Disarmament: Its Politics and Economics*. Boston: American Academy of Arts and Sciences, 1962. Fourteen experts comment on the primary issues related to peace through disarmament.
15. Nilsen, Thomas R., ed. *Essays on Rhetorical Criticism*. New York: Random House, 1968. The essays in this volume explore the scope of contemporary writing on rhetorical criticism from philosophical, literary, sociological, and experimental perspectives.
16. Pool, Ithiel de Sola. *Communication and Values in Relation to War and Peace*. New York: Institute for International Order, 1961. This is

a listing of forty-four possible research projects for determining the role world opinion makers play in promoting world peace.

17. Ramsey, Paul. *War and the Christian Conscience*. Durham, N.C.: Duke University Press, 1961. Ramsey argues that the doctrine of a just war is applicable in the 1960s and that to depart from it is to surrender to irrationality and gross immorality.
18. Steel, Ronald. *Pax Americana*. New York: Viking Press, 1967. After making a detailed critique of American foreign policy for the last twenty years, Steel calls for America to turn away from global fantasies and to the work of perfecting the human race within its own frontiers.
19. Stonier, Tom. *Nuclear Disaster*. Cleveland: World Publishing Co., 1964. Armed with numerous statistics, Stonier attempts to estimate the immediate and long-range impact which the burst of a twenty-megaton thermonuclear weapon on Manhattan Island would have upon New York.
20. Waskow, Arthur I. *The Worried Man's Guide to World Peace*. Garden City, N.Y.: Doubleday, 1963. In a superior one-volume treatment Waskow describes the complexities facing policy makers and citizens who wish to take an active role in promoting world peace.

PART ONE

SCIENTISTS AND POLITICS

I

CHARLES P. SNOW

The Moral Un-Neutrality of Science

In 1960 Sir Charles P. Snow retired after fifteen years as Commissioner of Civil Service for the British government and came to America to lecture for a year on problems related to science and government. His distinguished careers in science, literature, and government have made him an effective spokesman on questions of peace. From 1930 to 1950 he pursued his first career as a physicist at Christ's College, Cambridge. Beginning his literary career with a detective novel in 1932, Sir Charles has concentrated in recent years on exploring the lives of modern scientists in a series of nine novels called *Strangers and Brothers.* In 1962 he became Lord Rector of St. Andrews University.

His rise to international prominence came after publication of *The Two Cultures and the Scientific Revolution,* a series of lectures delivered at Cambridge University in 1959. In these addresses he argued that Western society was troubled by a growing chasm between its literary intellectuals and its scientists.[1]

Early in December 1960, Sir Charles gave the Godkin

Reprinted from Science, CXXXIII (January 27, 1961), 256–259, by permission from Sir Charles P. Snow and the American Association for the Advancement of Science.

[1] C. P. Snow, *The Two Cultures and the Scientific Revolution* (Cambridge, Mass.: Cambridge University Press, 1959), pp. 3–6.

lectures at Harvard University.[2] On December 27 he delivered the speech included here to members of the American Association for the Advancement of Science during its annual meeting. This address differs considerably from others included in this volume: the speaker is an Englishman addressing a group of American scientists on a topic of mutual concern; the speech was ostensibly to be a lecture but is actually a persuasive plea for scientists to be more conscious of their involvement in moral questions. Moreover, Father Theodore M. Hesburgh, president of the University of Notre Dame, and William O. Baker, president for research at the Bell Telephone Laboratories, shared the platform with Sir Charles, each giving a brief speech in response to his arguments.

Sir Charles' prediction that between 1960 and 1970 some nuclear bombs would explode "through accident, or folly, or madness" received widespread attention in the English and American press.

Scientists are the most important occupational group in the world today. At this moment, what they do is of passionate concern to the whole of human society. At this moment, the scientists have little influence on the world effect of what they do. Yet, potentially, they can have great influence. The rest of the world is frightened both of what they do—that is, of the intellectual discoveries of science—and of its effect. The rest of the world, transferring its fears, is frightened of the scientists themselves and tends to think of them as radically different from other men.

As an ex-scientist, if I may call myself so, I know that is nonsense. I have even tried to express in fiction some kinds of scientific temperament and scientific experience. I know well enough that scientists are very much like other men. After all, we are all human, even if some of us don't give that appear-

[2] These lectures were published in *Science and Government* (Cambridge, Mass.: Harvard University Press, 1960). Sir Charles replied to criticisms of the lectures in *A Postscript to Science and Government* (Cambridge, Mass.: Harvard University Press, 1962).

ance. I think I would be prepared to risk a generalization. The scientists I have known (and because of my official life I have known as many as anyone in the world) have been in certain respects just perceptibly more morally admirable than most other groups of intelligent men.

That is a sweeping statement, and I mean it only in a statistical sense. But I think there is just a little in it. The moral qualities I admire in scientists are quite simple ones, but I am very suspicious of attempts to oversubtilize moral qualities. It is nearly always a sign, not of true sophistication, but of a specific kind of triviality. So I admire in scientists very simple virtues—like courage, truth-telling, kindness—in which, judged by the low standards which the rest of us manage to achieve, the scientists are not deficient. I think on the whole the scientists make slightly better husbands and fathers than most of us, and I admire them for it. I don't know the figures, and I should be curious to have them sorted out, but I am prepared to bet that the proportion of divorces among scientists is slightly but significantly less than that among other groups of similar education and income. I do not apologize for considering that a good thing.[3]

A close friend of mine is a very distinguished scientist. He is also one of the few scientists I know who has lived what we used to call a Bohemian life. When we were both younger, he thought he would undertake historical research to see how many great scientists had been as fond of women as he was. I think he would have felt mildly supported if he could have found a precedent. I remember his reporting to me that his researches hadn't had any luck. The really great scientists seemed to vary from a few neutral characters to a large number who were depressingly "normal." The only gleam of comfort was to be found in the life of Jerome Cardan; and Cardan wasn't anything like enough to outweigh all the others.

So scientists are not much different from other men. They are certainly no worse than other men. But they do differ from other men in one thing. That is the point I started with. Whether they like it or not, what they do is of critical impor-

[3] What image is Snow trying to create for the scientist in this and the preceding paragraph?

tance for the human race. Intellectually, it has transformed the climate of our time. Socially, it will decide whether we live or die, and how we live or die. It holds decisive powers for good and evil. *That* is the situation in which the scientists find themselves. They may not have asked for it, or may only have asked for it in part, but they cannot escape it. They think, many of the more sensitive of them, that they don't deserve to have this weight of responsibility heaved upon them. All they want to do is to get on with their work. I sympathize. But the scientists can't escape the responsibility—any more than they, or the rest of us, can escape the gravity of the moment in which we stand.

There is of course one way to contract out. It has been a favorite way for intellectual persons caught in the midst of water too rough for them.

It consists of the invention of categories—or, if you like, of the division of moral labor. That is, the scientists who want to contract out say, *we* produce the tools. *We* stop there. It is for *you*—the rest of the world, the politicians—to say how the tools are used. The tools may be used for purposes which most of us would regard as bad. If so, we are sorry. But as scientists, that is no concern of ours.

This is the doctrine of the ethical neutrality of science. I can't accept it for an instant. I don't believe any scientist of serious feeling can accept it. It is hard, some think, to find the precise statements which will prove it wrong. Yet we nearly all feel intuitively that the invention of comfortable categories is a moral trap. It is one of the easier methods of letting the conscience rust. It is exactly what the early 19th century economists, such as Ricardo, did in the face of the facts of the first industrial revolution. We wonder now how men, intelligent men, can have been so morally blind. We realize how the exposure of that moral blindness gave Marxism its apocalyptic force. We are now, in the middle of the scientific or second industrial revolution, in something like the same position as Ricardo.[4] Are we going to let our consciences rust? Can we

[4] Snow has used an argument from analogy to support his assertion against the ethical neutrality of science. Is this an effective strategy?

ignore that intimation we nearly all have, that scientists have a unique responsibility? Can we believe it, that science is morally neutral?

To me—it would be dishonest to pretend otherwise—there is only one answer to those questions. Yet I have been brought up in the presence of the same intellectual categories as most western scientists. It would also be dishonest to pretend that I find it easy to construct a rationale which expresses what I now believe. The best I can hope for is to fire a few sighting shots. Perhaps someone who sees more clearly than I can will come along and make a real job of it.

Let me begin with a remark which seems some way off the point. Anyone who has ever worked in any science knows how much esthetic joy he has obtained. That is, in the actual *activity* of science, in the process of making a discovery, however humble it is, one can't help feeling an awareness of beauty. The subjective experience, the esthetic satisfaction, seems exactly the same as the satisfaction one gets from writing a poem or a novel, or composing a piece of music. I don't think anyone has succeeded in distinguishing between them. The literature of scientific discovery is full of this esthetic joy. The very best communication of it that I know comes in G. H. Hardy's book, *A Mathematician's Apology*. Graham Greene once said he thought that, along with Henry James's prefaces, this was the best account of the artistic experience ever written. But one meets the same thing throughout the history of science. Bolyai's great yell of triumph when he saw he could construct a self-consistent, non-Euclidean geometry; Rutherford's revelation to his colleagues that he knew what the atom was like; Darwin's slow, patient, timorous certainty that at last he had got there—all these are voices, different voices, of esthetic ecstasy.

That is not the end of it. The *result* of the activity of science, the actual finished piece of scientific work, has an esthetic value in itself. The judgments passed on it by other scientists will more often than not be expressed in esthetic terms: "That's beautiful!" or "That really is very pretty!" (as the understating English tend to say). The esthetics of scientific constructs, like the esthetics of works of art, are variegated. We think some of the great syntheses, like Newton's, beautiful because of their classical simplicity, but we see a different kind of beauty in the relativistic extension of the wave equation or the interpretation of the structure of deoxyribonucleic acid, perhaps because of the touch of unexpectedness. Scientists know their kinds of beauty when they see them.[5] They are suspicious, and scientific history shows they have always been right to have been so, when a subject is in an "ugly" state. For example, most physicists feel in their bones that the present bizarre assembly of nuclear particles, as grotesque as a stamp collection, can't possibly be, in the long run, the last word.

We should not restrict the esthetic values to what we call "pure" science. Applied science has its beauties, which are, in my view, identical in nature. The magnetron has been a marvelously useful device, but it was a beautiful device, not exactly apart from its utility but because it did, with such supreme economy, precisely what it was designed to do. Right down in the field of development, the esthetic experience is as real to engineers. When they forget it, when they begin to design heavy-power equipment about twice as heavy as it needs to be, engineers are the first to know that they are lacking virtue.

There is no doubt, then, about the esthetic content of science, both in the activity and the result. But esthetics has no connection with morals, say the categorizers. I don't want to waste time on peripheral issues—but are you quite sure of that? Or is it possible that these categories are inventions to make us evade the human and social conditions in which we now exist? But let us move straight on to something else, which is right in the grain of the activity of science and which is at the same time quintessentially moral. I mean, the desire to find the truth.[6]

[5] What effect does Snow's discussion of beauty have upon his attempt to humanize scientists?

[6] This paragraph serves as an effective bridge between the two main points of the speech. What kinds of sentences are used to make this a smooth transition?

By *truth,* I don't intend anything complicated, once again. I am using the word as a scientist uses it. We all know that the philosophical examination of the concept of empirical truth gets us into some curious complexities, but most scientists really don't care. They know that the truth, as they use the word and as the rest of us use it in the language of common speech, is what makes science work. That is good enough for them. On it rests the whole great edifice of modern science. They have a sneaking sympathy for Rutherford, who, when asked to examine the philosophical bases of science, was inclined to reply, as he did to the metaphysician Samuel Alexander: "Well, what have you been talking all your life, Alexander? Just hot air! Nothing but hot air!"

Anyway, truth in their own straightforward sense is what the scientists are trying to find. They want to find what is *there.* Without that desire, there is no science. It is the driving force of the whole activity. It compels the scientist to have an overriding respect for truth, every stretch of the way. That is, if you're going to find what is *there,* you mustn't deceive yourself or anyone else. You mustn't lie to yourself. At the crudest level, you mustn't fake your experiments.

Curiously enough, scientists do try to behave like that. A short time ago, I wrote a novel in which the story hinged on a case of scientific fraud. But I made one of my characters, who was himself a very good scientist, say that, considering the opportunities and temptations, it is astonishing how few such cases there are. We have all heard of perhaps half a dozen open and notorious ones, which are on the record for anyone to read—ranging from the "discovery" of the L radiation to the singular episode of the Piltdown man.

We have all, if we have lived any time in the scientific world, heard private talk of something like another dozen cases which for various reasons are not yet public property. In some cases, we know the motives for the cheating—sometimes, but not always, sheer personal advantage, such as getting money or a job. But not always. A special kind of vanity has led more than one man into scientific faking. At a lower level of research, there are presumably some more cases. There must have been occasional Ph.D. students who scraped by with the help of a bit of fraud.

But the total number of all these men is vanishingly small by the side of the total number of scientists. Incidentally, the effect on science of such frauds is also vanishingly small. Science is a self-correcting system. That is, no fraud (or honest mistake) is going to stay undetected for long. There is no need for an extrinsic scientific criticism, because criticism is inherent in the process itself. So that all that a fraud can do is waste the time of the scientists who have to clear it up.

The remarkable thing is not the handful of scientists who deviate from the search for truth but the overwhelming numbers who keep to it. That is a demonstration, absolutely clear for anyone to see, of moral behavior on a very large scale.

We take it for granted. Yet it is very important. It differentiates science in its widest sense (which includes scholarship) from all other intellectual activities. There is a built-in moral component right in the core of the scientific activity itself. The desire to find the truth is itself a moral impulse, or at least contains a moral impulse. The way in which a scientist tries to find the truth imposes on him a constant moral discipline. We say a scientific conclusion—such as the contradiction of parity by Lee and Yang—is "true" in the limited sense of scientific truth, just as we say that it is "beautiful" according to the criteria of scientific esthetics. We also know that to reach this conclusion took a set of actions which would have been useless without the moral nature. That is, all through the marvelous experiments of Wu and her colleagues, there was the constant moral exercise of seeking and telling the truth. To scientists, who are brought up in this climate, this seems as natural as breathing. Yet it is a wonderful thing. Even if the scientific activity contained only this one moral component, that alone would be enough to let us say that it was morally un-neutral.[7]

But is this the only moral component? All scientists would agree about the beauty and the truth. In the western world,

[7] Has Snow presented enough arguments to expect his audience of scientists to accept his conclusion?

they wouldn't agree on much more. Some will feel with me in what I am going to say. Some will not. That doesn't affect me much, except that I am worried by the growth of an attitude I think very dangerous, a kind of technological conformity disguised as cynicism. I shall say a little more about that later. As for disagreement, G. H. Hardy used to comment that a serious man ought not to waste his time stating a majority opinion—there are plenty of others to do that. That was the voice of classical scientific nonconformity. I wish that we heard it more often.

Let me cite some grounds for hope. Any of us who were working in science before 1933 can remember what the atmosphere was like. It is a terrible bore when aging men in their fifties speak about the charms of their youth. Yet I am going to irritate you—just as Talleyrand irritated his juniors—by saying that unless one was on the scene before 1933, one hasn't known the sweetness of the scientific life. The scientific world of the twenties was as near to being a full-fledged international community as we are likely to get. Don't think I'm saying that the men involved were superhuman or free from the ordinary frailties. That wouldn't come well from me, who have spent a fraction of my writing life pointing out that scientists are, first and foremost, men. But the atmosphere of the twenties in science was filled with an air of benevolence and magnanimity which transcended the people who lived in it.

Anyone who ever spent a week in Cambridge or Göttingen or Copenhagen felt it all round him. Rutherford had very human faults, but he was a great man with abounding human generosity. For him the world of science was a world that lived on a plane above the nation-state, and lived there with joy. That was at least as true of those two other great men, Niels Bohr and Franck, and some of that spirit rubbed off on to the pupils round them. The same was true of the Roman school of physics.

The personal links within this international world were very close. It is worth remembering that Peter Kapitza, who was a loyal Soviet citizen, honored my country by working in Rutherford's laboratory for many years. He became a fellow of the Royal Society, a fellow of Trinity College, Cambridge, and the founder and kingpin of the best physics club Cambridge has known. He never gave up his Soviet citizenship and is now director of the Institute of Physical Problems in Moscow. Through him a generation of English scientists came to have personal knowledge of their Russian colleagues. These exchanges were then, and have remained, more valuable than all the diplomatic exchanges ever invented.

The Kapitza phenomenon couldn't take place now. I hope to live to see the day when a young Kapitza can once more work for 16 years in Berkeley or Cambridge and then go back to an eminent place in his own country. When that can happen, we are all right. But after the idyllic years of world science, we passed into a tempest of history, and, by an unfortunate coincidence, we passed into a technological tempest too.

The discovery of atomic fission broke up the world of international physics. "This has killed a beautiful subject," said Mark Oliphant, the father figure of Australian physics, in 1945, after the bombs had dropped. In intellectual terms, he has not turned out to be right. In spiritual and moral terms, I sometimes think he has.

A good deal of the international community of science remains in other fields—in great areas of biology, for example. Many biologists are feeling the identical liberation, the identical joy at taking part in a magnanimous enterprise, that physicists felt in the twenties. It is more than likely that the moral and intellectual leadership of science will pass to biologists, and it is among them that we shall find the Rutherfords, Bohrs, and Francks of the next generation.

Physicists have had a bitterer task. With the discovery of fission, and with some technical breakthroughs in electronics, physicists became, almost overnight, the most important military resource a nation-state could call on. A large number of physicists became soldiers not in uniform.[8] So they have remained, in the advanced societies, ever since.

[8] Observe in the next five paragraphs how Snow repeats his reference to scientists as soldiers. How does this affect his argument against moral neutrality?

It is very difficult to see what else they could have done. All this began in the Hitler war. Most scientists thought then that Nazism was as near absolute evil as a human society can manage. I myself thought so. I still think so, without qualification. That being so, Nazism had to be fought, and since the Nazis might make fission bombs—which we thought possible until 1944, and which was a continual nightmare if one was remotely in the know—well, then, we had to make them too. Unless one was an unlimited pacifist, there was nothing else to do. And unlimited pacificism is a position which most of us cannot sustain.

Therefore I respect, and to a large extent share, the moral attitudes of those scientists who devoted themselves to making the bomb. But the trouble is, when you get onto any kind of moral escalator, to know whether you're ever going to be able to get off. When scientists became soldiers they gave up something, so imperceptibly that they didn't realize it, of the full scientific life. Not intellectually. I see no evidence that scientific work on weapons of maximum destruction has been in any intellectual respect different from other scientific work. But there is a moral difference.

It may be—scientists who are better men than I am often take this attitude, and I have tried to represent it faithfully in one of my books—that this is a moral price which, in certain circumstances, has to be paid. Nevertheless, it is no good pretending that there is not a moral price. Soldiers have to obey. That is the foundation of their morality. It is not the foundation of the scientific morality. Scientists have to question and if necessary to rebel. I don't want to be misunderstood. I am no anarchist. I am not suggesting that loyalty is not a prime virtue. I am not saying that all rebellion is good. But I am saying that loyalty can easily turn into conformity, and that conformity can often be a cloak for the timid and self-seeking. So can obedience, carried to the limit. When you think of the long and gloomy history of man, you will find that far more, and far more hideous, crimes have been committed in the name of obedience than have ever been committed in the name of rebellion. If you doubt that, read William Shirer's *Rise and Fall of the Third Reich.* The German officer corps were brought up in the most rigorous code of obedience. To them, no more honorable and God-fearing body of men could conceivably exist. Yet in the name of obedience, they were party to, and assisted in, the most wicked large-scale actions in the history of the world.

Scientists must not go that way. Yet the duty to question is not much of a support when you are living in the middle of an organized society. I speak with feeling here. I was an official for 20 years. I went into official life at the beginning of the war, for the reasons that prompted my scientific friends to begin to make weapons. I stayed in that life until a year ago, for the same reason that made my scientific friends turn into civilian soldiers. The official's life in England is not quite so disciplined as a soldier's, but it is very nearly so. I think I know the virtues, which are very great, of the men who live that disciplined life. I also know what for me was the moral trap. I, too, had got onto an escalator. I can put the result in a sentence: I was coming to hide behind the institution; I was losing the power to say no.

Only a very bold man, when he is a member of an organized society, can keep the power to say no. I tell you that, not being a very bold man, or one who finds it congenial to stand alone, away from his colleagues. We can't expect many scientists to do it. Is there any tougher ground for them to stand on? I suggest to you that there is. I believe that there is a spring of moral action in the scientific activity which is at least as strong as the search for truth. The name of this spring is *knowledge*. Scientists *know* certain things in a fashion more immediate and more certain than those who don't comprehend what science is. Unless we are abnormally weak or abnormally wicked men, this knowledge is bound to shape our actions. Most of us are timid, but to an extent, knowledge gives us guts. Perhaps it can give us guts strong enough for the jobs in hand.

I had better take the most obvious example. All physical scientists *know* that it is relatively easy to make plutonium. We know this, not as a journalistic fact at second hand, but as a fact in our own experience. We can work out the number of scientific and engineering personnel needed for a nation-state to equip itself with fission and fusion bombs. We *know* that, for a dozen or more states, it will only take perhaps six years, perhaps less. Even the best informed of us always exaggerate these periods.

This we know, with the certainty of—what shall I call it?—engineering truth. We also—most of us—are familiar with statistics and the nature of odds. We know, with the certainty of statistical truth, that if enough of these weapons are made, by enough different states, some of them are going to blow up, through accident, or folly, or madness—the motives don't matter. What does matter is the nature of the statistical fact.

All this we *know*. We know it in a more direct sense than any politician because it comes from our direct experience. It is part of our minds. Are we going to let it happen?

All this we *know*. It throws upon scientists a direct and personal responsibility. It is not enough to say that scientists have a responsibility as citizens. They have a much greater one than that, and one different in kind. For scientists have a moral imperative to say what they know. It is going to make them unpopular in their own nation-states. It may do worse than make them unpopular. That doesn't matter. Or at least, it does matter to you and me, but it must not count in the face of the risks.

For we genuinely know the risks. We are faced with an either-or, and we haven't much time. The *either* is acceptance of a restriction of nuclear armaments. This is going to begin, just as a token, with an agreement on the stopping of nuclear tests. The United States is not going to get the 99.9-percent "security" that it has been asking for. This is unobtainable, though there are other bargains that the United States could probably secure. I am not going to conceal from you that this course involves certain risks. They are quite obvious, and no honest man is going to blink them. That is the *either*. The *or* is not a risk but a certainty. It is this. There is no agreement on tests. The nuclear arms race between the United States and the U.S.S.R. not only continues but accelerates. Other countries join in. Within, at the most, six years, China and several other states have a stock of nuclear bombs. Within, at the most, ten years, some of those bombs are going off. I am saying this as responsibly as I can. *That* is the certainty. On the one side, therefore, we have a finite risk. On the other side we have a certainty of disaster. Between a risk and a certainty, a sane man does not hesitate.[9]

It is the plain duty of scientists to explain this either-or. It is a duty which seems to me to come from the moral nature of the scientific activity itself.

The same duty, though in a much more pleasant form, arises with respect to the benevolent powers of science. For scientists know, and again with the certainty of scientific knowledge, that we possess every scientific fact we need to transform the physical life of half the world. And transform it within the span of people now living. I mean, we have all the resources to help half the world live as long as we do and eat enough. All that is missing is the will. We *know* that. Just as we know that you in the United States, and to a slightly lesser extent we in the United Kingdom, have been almost unimaginably lucky. We are sitting like people in a smart and cozy restaurant and we are eating comfortably, looking out of the window into the streets. Down on the pavement are people who are looking up at us, people who by chance have different colored skins from ours, and are rather hungry. Do you wonder that they don't like us all that much? Do you wonder that we sometimes feel ashamed of ourselves, as we look out through that plate glass?

Well, it is within our power to get started on that problem. We are morally impelled to. We all know that, if the human species does solve that one, there will be consequences which are themselves problems. For instance, the population of the world will become embarrassingly large. But that is another challenge. There are going to be challenges to our intelligence and to our moral nature as long as man remains man. After all, a challenge is not, as the word is coming to be used, an excuse for slinking off and doing nothing. A challenge is something to be picked up.

[9] This is the major argument of Snow's speech. Why is it stated here instead of as the first point in his speech?

For all these reasons, I believe the world community of scientists has a final responsibility upon it—a greater responsibility than is pressing on any other body of men. I do not pretend to know how they will bear this responsibility. These may be famous last words, but I have an inextinguishable hope. For, as I have said, there is no doubt that the scientific activity is both beautiful and truthful. I cannot prove it, but I believe that, simply because scientists cannot escape their own knowledge, they also won't be able to avoid showing themselves disposed to good.

CRITICAL ANALYSIS AND PROJECTS

1. Snow's treatment of esthetic joy is a good illustration of how a speaker can develop a point. What rhetorical device does he use?
2. A speaker often uses personal pronouns to achieve rapport with his audience and to impart directness to the speech. Does Snow's labeling of himself in the second paragraph as an "ex-scientist" and his later use of "we" or "they" in reference to scientists confuse the listener? Would the consistent use of "we" have improved the tone of his speech?
3. What devices does Snow employ to make his ideas vivid? What effect would his use of more figures like "letting the conscience rust," "soldiers not in uniform," and "moral escalator" have had on his arguments?
4. Prepare a short speech in which you support or challenge Snow's prediction that "statistical truth" assures us that some atomic bombs will explode in the near future. See items 3. and 4. in the bibliography.
5. Select a prominent scientist, perhaps one of those named by Snow, and prepare a brief speech in which you show his response to the challenge of moral responsibility.

SELECTED BIBLIOGRAPHY

1. Davis, Robert G. *C. P. Snow.* New York: Columbia University Press, 1965.
2. Karl, Frederick R. *C. P. Snow: The Politics of Conscience.* Carbondale, Ill.: Southern Illinois University Press, 1963.

3. Larus, Joel. *Nuclear Weapons Safety and the Common Defense*. Columbus, Ohio: Ohio State University Press, 1967.
4. Lilienthal, David E. *Change, Hope, and the Bomb*. Princeton, N.J.: Princeton University Press, 1963.
5. Pauling, Linus. "Peace on Earth: The Position of the Scientists," *Bulletin of Atomic Scientists,* XXIII (October 1967) , 46–48.
6. Thale, Jerome. *C. P. Snow*. New York: Scribner, 1963.
7. Weintraub, Stanley. *C. P. Snow: A Spectrum: Science-Criticism-Fiction*. New York: Scribner, 1963.
8. Wiesner, Jerome B. *Where Science and Politics Meet*. New York: McGraw-Hill, 1965.

II

EDWARD TELLER

Peace Through Civil Defense

Although there are few scientists as controversial as Edward Teller, he has been praised as "one of the most original, imaginative, and versatile scientists in the world today."[1] Forced to flee the Nazi tyranny of his native Hungary in the 1930s, Teller taught at the University of London and later came to the United States in 1935 as professor of physics at George Washington University. He became an American citizen in 1941.

His long and controversial involvement in military affairs began in 1939 when he and five other scientists persuaded Albert Einstein to write his famous letter to President Roosevelt which resulted in the Manhattan Project. From 1941 to 1946 Teller assisted in the development of the atomic bomb and in 1950, despite much scientific and political opposition, he initiated the crash program that permitted the United States to develop the first hydrogen bomb. He has taught physics at the University of Chicago and the University of California at Berkeley and is currently director of the

Reprinted from a revised manuscript of the speech given by Dr. Edward Teller to the Commonwealth Club of California, San Francisco, December 13, 1961. Printed by permission of Dr. Edward Teller and *Vital Speeches of the Day*.

[1] Statement by the Enrico Fermi Award Selection Committee quoted in Eugene Wigner, "Fermi Award: AEC Honors Teller for Contributions to Nuclear Science," *Science*, CXXXVIII (December 7, 1962), 1087.

Lawrence Radiation Laboratory, Livermore, California.

Teller believes that the safety of the West lies in full military preparedness and continued development of nuclear weapons until a "supranational" authority is built "which has moral strength and physical strength to maintain peace."

He has frequently presented his views to Senate subcommittees and defended his position in debates with those who oppose him.[2] After witnessing his attack upon the nuclear test-ban treaty, one Senator described him as "John L. Lewis, John Barrymore, and Billy Sunday all in one."[3] His tenacity caused a colleague to remark, "Only a sincere man will put his head on the chopping block as often as he does. Just as often he's been vindicated."[4]

Prior to the general reduction in East-West tensions in 1963, fallout shelters were much debated as a system for protecting the country from nuclear attacks. In the speech included here Teller stresses the role of civil defense in preventing war. His arguments for fallout shelters were delivered four months after the Berlin crisis and three months after the Soviets had resumed nuclear testing in the atmosphere. Under these circumstances public interest and debate about fallout shelters grew rapidly in 1961. Early in the year, for instance, individual requests to government agencies for civil defense literature ran about 4,700 a month. By September the requests had jumped to 6,500 a day.

Teller's speech was designed to answer specific arguments against fallout shelters found in an address delivered to the same audience a month earlier by Gerard Piel, publisher of *Scientific American,* and to convince his listeners that the construction of shelters would enhance rather than hinder the chances for peace.

[2] See, for example, his encounter with Linus Pauling in *Teller-Pauling Debate: Fallout and Disarmament,* a film produced by KQED, San Francisco, California, and available through NET Film Services, Indiana University, Bloomington, Indiana.

[3] *Newsweek,* LXII (September 2, 1963), 22.

[4] *Ibid.* See, for instance, "An Answer to Teller," *Saturday Evening Post,* CCXXXV (April 14, 1962), 69–74.

You heard a few moments ago the most interesting enumeration of recent important events. It was the gratifying news that today this club had 10,000 members and can speak with 10,000 voices. I am afraid it has also the capability of listening with 20,000 ears which is somewhat frightening to me!

About a month ago Gerard Piel made an important contribution, in this place, to civil defense, a very significant phase of our preparedness.

He said a few things that needed to be said: that civil defense cannot be simply the building of fallout shelters; that there are dangers from blast and from fire which are as great or greater than the danger from fallout. He is right.

He also said the two alternatives—red or dead—must not be the only ones. He certainly is correct.[5]

Now, my purpose in my main day-to-day work—and in talking to you—is to make a little contribution toward another and a reasonable alternative. My main purpose is to find a way in which we can have peace and in which we can preserve our freedom. This will not be easy, and I do not know the answer, but I have strong feelings about the direction to look for an answer.

I also have the complete conviction that any simple answer is not the right one. And here I disagree with Mr. Piel when he puts the problem in an exaggerated and simplified form.[6]

He said that real civil defense will mean that the nation will have to go underground; and he continued: "The down payment on the cost of taking the nation underground would be $150 billion. But that is only the fiscal cost. The social cost of going underground would not fall short of the total transformation of our way of life, the suspension of our civil institutions, the habituation of our people to violence and the ultimate militarization of our society."

That figure $150 billion is grossly and improperly exaggerated. The statements which follow it are even more wrong.

[5] What is the effect of Teller's decision to tell his audience where he agrees with Piel before presenting his own case?

[6] A common practice in argumentative discourse is to accuse your opponent of exaggerating and oversimplifying a problem. Does Teller prove these charges against Piel?

Mr. Piel considers civil defense as a form of violence. He says it is a step toward this ever-growing danger, the escalation of military force, and he says: "This is a sinister development because it works a psychological subversion of both government and citizenry."

These are strong words. If civil defense is violence, what is active defense? What is our whole military establishment together with the development of missiles and of nuclear explosives? Knowing that Mr. Piel is a reasonable and logical person, I know he must be opposed to all of these.

That we are in danger—that we have to try to preserve peace—we are all agreed. There is a disagreement as to the question: From what quarter does our main danger arise? There are those—and Mr. Piel is one—who believe the main danger comes from the military men in the United States as well as in Russia, and the peace-loving people on both sides of the Iron Curtain can stop this dreadful trend which may carry us towards all-out war.

There are others who believe differently—and I am one of them. I believe that, with the exception of a completely insignificant minority, we are all peace-loving and this includes our military men—many of whom I know and respect very highly. I also believe with Mr. Piel that there are a great majority of peace-loving people behind the Iron Curtain, but I believe—in fact, I think I know—that these peace-loving people behind the Iron Curtain have no voice; and the minority, in Russia, is determined to conquer the world. And there are some leaders who love peace only to the extent that they would rather conquer us without bloodshed and without risk. In fact, I believe that they are cautious and will not attack us as long as we are strong.

We must be both strong and patient; we must never strike first, but we must be able to retaliate in case we are attacked, and furthermore, we must be able to survive an attack so that it would become clear to the Russian leaders that by attacking us they cannot win.

If we accomplish this, we shall be safe—but it will take a lot to accomplish this.

I do not believe that civil defense is a panacea. It will be hard to have a good civil defense, but it is necessary and possible. Mr. Piel had a point, but he exaggerated it.

Past expenditures on civil defense, amounting to less than 1/10th of a cent out of each tax dollar, have indeed been insignificant. At present, this amount has been stepped up to 3/10th of a cent out of each tax dollar. This is a good beginning, but still not sufficient. What we need is perhaps 10% of our military budget—$4 billion a year spent reasonably over a series of years. I believe the Russians today are not strong enough to attack us. I believe that if we start to work on civil defense today, then they never will be in a position to attack us. But if we neglect civil defense, we are exposing ourselves to a deadly danger.

Now, specifically, Mr. Piel has told you that there are great dangers in the neighborhood of a nuclear bomb against which he said there is no defense. These dangers are blast and fire. These dangers are great but to say that there is no defense against them is incorrect.

The defense is expensive—but not very expensive. If you do your best with appropriately constructed mass shelters, you can buy reasonable defense for approximately $200 per person. This can be done by excavating tunnels underground and by building into these tunnels Quonset hut-like structures. This has been worked out by the Naval radiological defense people here in San Francisco. It is believed—and I think correctly—that such a shelter will stand up under a multi-megaton explosion if that explosion is farther away than approximately one mile.

There will not be much warning. A missile takes only 20 minutes to get here if it starts from Russia. It is necessary that mass shelters be available to everyone, within five minutes' walking distance. In heavily built-up areas this is possible.

Nor is this Quonset hut structure the only possibility. Where you have limestone or other soft rock formation, you can dig straight into the rock and have an even more adequate shelter for approximately the same cost per person. In places distant from the target area, less complete shelter will be adequate.

The danger of fallout has somehow been exaggerated out of

all proportion. The statement often repeated by Mr. Piel and others, that there will be a danger to future generations, is grossly distorted.

I have estimated that a really terrible attack will, among other things, increase the normal mutation rate for one generation by a factor of two. There will be twice as many still births and twice as many changes as under normal conditions. Mutations have also contributed to the development of the living world; if a natural process is speeded up by a factor of two for one generation, it is not something you would want, but it is certainly not a catastrophe compared to this horrible possibility of an all-out war.[7] Let's please see things in proportion.

The fire danger, however, is very real. The Russian multimegaton bomb—50 megatons, 100 megatons—could be exploded in such a way as to produce a great amount of fire. How much fire will depend to a great extent on how much combustible material is around. Fires can be fought. Against fire there is a defense in well-constructed underground shelters. One should add chemicals to absorb the carbon dioxide, and bottled oxygen (which for mass shelters is not very expensive) to supply air for the probable maximum duration of the fire, which may be twenty-four hours. This will make the defense complete not only against nuclear attack but against chemical and biological attack as well.

Please do not interpret my words as a statement which is authoritatively correct—which presents a real plan. The civil defense program is of enormous complexity, and so far we have not taken it seriously enough. I am merely saying that if you use your imagination, not only to outline the danger but also to find every reasonable avenue to combat this danger, solutions can be found, and we can even discern the beginnings of such a solution. That is all I claim.

Mr. Piel brought up another point of extremely great importance. When we come out of the shelter, then what? How much of the nation's livelihood will have been de-

[7] What is your assessment of Teller's attempt to use personal opinion to refute the radiation hazard?

stroyed? Mr. Piel says maybe half or two thirds. This is possible. In many essential areas all our wealth may be destroyed. Some of you may know that all our wealth amounts to the national income of only three years. If we preserve a sensible organization, and if we store some goods against a rainy day, so that we won't starve, and won't have to start the rebuilding processes with our ten bare fingers, we can, after a number of austere but not necessarily terrible years, rebuild our country to its old strength, and to a better strength.

To do this will be even more difficult than planning the shelters, but we have an important asset. We have food surpluses which can last for two years. These food surpluses may be destroyed if left in an insecure place. If they are put into safe places and if they are distributed throughout the country near processing facilities, or in a semiprocessed form, we can be sure that we at least will eat while we rebuild the country. And if we have built the shelters, the great majority of our population can be saved—even under the most savage and sudden attack.[8]

We throw away our machines when we can think of something better. Some of these machines should be mothballed so we should have something to start from if attacked. Civil defense and planning for recovery are possible in a rich country with surpluses like the United States. This same thing is infinitely more difficult in Russia, struggling to establish its first-generation industry. They have no surpluses. They run their machines until the machines fall apart.

The Russians can be convinced that in case of all-out war our country will survive—and we can recover faster than they can. Under these conditions we can be sure they will not attack first.

In making ourselves safe for the next few years, we will have bought time. Its value depends on what we do with it. The right plan for a peaceful world will not help us, if we have no strength to defend ourselves. Our military strength will be of

[8] What effect would the use of specific figures showing how many Americans might survive a nuclear attack have had upon Teller's point concerning the value of shelters?

no avail if we do not know how to construct a peaceful, stable order on this world, which decade by decade becomes more closely interrelated and, therefore, if anarchic, more dangerous.

Recently we have made a very important step toward construction of a more stable world. We have announced publicly that we shall never strike first. We must behave in such a way that an all-out war will never be, and need never be, started by the United States. If we are strong, an all-out war will not be started by the other side either.

This does not mean that we shall take every Russian aggression without resistance. We must develop a policy, and we can, which will resist Russian aggression in every place, at any time, on the same scale on which this aggression is committed. If we can act according to these principles, we will have made another important step toward lasting peace.

But the real question is: How can we construct a lawful, peaceful family of nations? We can be quite sure that the Russians, who are bent on world conquest, will not sit down with us at the negotiating table and will not give up their plan to conquer the world merely because we ask them to do so. We must first develop strength and the unity in the Free World, and this will take a decade or two at least.

If the Russians are convinced—if they will be convinced in the future—that they cannot conquer the world without a devastating war, then may be the time, in a different situation from the present, to see how in a gradual and reasonable way we can begin to agree with them. We first have to stop them, and in order to do that we need unity. We need unity in the Free World. We must begin to build a supranational authority which has the moral strength and physical strength to maintain peace, and which has the power to help the backward nations in their struggle for a better existence.

If we take the full responsibility for a developing world in which the industrial revolution, and a better way of living, is spreading from continent to continent; if in this world we can become leaders; if we can make good on our own statements that all men are created equal whether in North or South America, or Africa, or Asia; if we can make good on these magnificent ideas and promises; and if we have the strength to safeguard ourselves and our friends while developing our world; then there will be real peace in our time.[9] And very important to this real safety and real peace, is this little, gentle contribution of civilian defense.

CRITICAL ANALYSIS AND PROJECTS

1. How does Teller win the attention of listeners and relate his topic to their interests?
2. Do you think the frequent references to Gerard Piel's arguments help or hinder Teller's case for fallout shelters? What is his major objection to Piel's position?
3. If used carefully, appeals to fear and economic gain can win a strong audience response. Read item 3. in the bibliography and then evaluate Teller's use of these appeals.
4. What effect does Teller's decision to include a discussion of future developments in American defense strategy have on the tone of the speech?
5. How would you describe the pattern of organization used by Teller? How could it be improved?
6. Read Piel's speech in *Vital Speeches,* XXVIII (February 1, 1962), 239–244, and determine which arguments Teller ignored. How important were they to the case against fallout shelters?
7. Study the literature on fallout shelters from 1961–1965 and prepare a speech indicating why most Americans decided not to build individual shelters.

SELECTED BIBLIOGRAPHY

1. Herr, David M. *After Nuclear Attack: A Demographic Inquiry*. New York: Frederick A. Praeger, 1965.
2. Glasstone, Samuel, ed. *The Effects of Nuclear Weapons*. Washington, D.C.: U.S. Government Printing Office, 1962.
3. Miller, Gerald R., and Murray A. Hewgill. "Some Recent Research on Fear-Arousing Message Appeals," *Speech Monographs,* XXXIII (November 1966), 377–391.

[9] Is this an effective style for a conclusion? How could it be improved?

4. Nathan, Otto, and Heinz Norden, eds. *Einstein on Peace.* New York: Simon and Schuster, 1960.
5. Stonier, Tom. *Nuclear Disaster.* Cleveland: World Publishing Co., 1964.
6. Teller, Edward. *The Reluctant Revolutionary.* Columbia, Mo.: University of Missouri Press, 1960.
7. ———, with Allen Brown. *The Legacy of Hiroshima.* Garden City, N.Y.: Doubleday, 1962.
8. ———, and Albert Latter. *Our Nuclear Future: Facts, Dangers and Opportunities.* New York: Criterion Books, 1958.

PART TWO

PEACE AND SECURITY

III

JOHN F. KENNEDY

The Strategy of Peace

During his first year in office President John F. Kennedy presented to the United Nations a request for general and complete disarmament under effective international control. Within a few months the crises in Berlin and Laos sabotaged his proposals. The following year the Cuban missile crisis nearly led to war between the United States and Russia, but from its ashes came the peace offensive of 1963.

In the late spring of 1963 President Kennedy made new preparations for an attempt to reach a détente with the Soviet Union. Late in May when a change in the mood of the Senate indicated increased support for a possible nuclear test-ban treaty, the President lost no time in asking his personal advisers to send their best thoughts on a peace address to his chief speech writer, Ted Sorensen.[1]

Since the Soviet Communist Party Central Committee would be meeting in mid-June and since President Kennedy planned a European trip later that month, the American University commencement speech, which he was already scheduled to give, seemed the perfect time and place for a major policy address. Accordingly, the President spoke on civil rights at the United States Mayors' Conference in Honolulu on June 9 and added the finishing touches to the Sorensen

Reprinted by permission from *Vital Speeches of the Day,* XXIX (July 1, 1963), 558–561.

[1] Arthur M. Schlesinger, Jr., *A Thousand Days: John F. Kennedy in the White House* (Boston: Houghton Mifflin Co., 1965), p. 900.

draft of the American University speech during the return flight to Washington.[2]

The speech accomplished its purpose. The Washington *Post* reacted with an editorial pointing out that it was vital to keep before the world a strong American plea for peaceful solutions to international problems and called the speech "another bid for an end to the cold war."[3] The Soviet press published the full text of the speech, and for the first time in many years a Russian translation broadcast by the Voice of America was not jammed.[4] In August 1963, the Nuclear Test-Ban Treaty was signed by the Soviet Union, the United Kingdom, and the United States. After bitter and prolonged debate Congress ratified the treaty in October 1963.

One year after this speech American University erected a monument to President Kennedy on the spot where he made his historic plea for peace.[5]

President [Hurst R.] Anderson, members of the faculty, board of trustees, my old colleague Senator Bob Byrd, who has earned his degree through many years of attending night law school while I am earning mine in the next 30 minutes, distinguished guests, ladies and gentlemen:[6]

It is with great pride that I participate in this ceremony of the American University sponsored by the Methodist Church, founded by Bishop John Fletcher Hurst and first opened by President Woodrow Wilson in 1914.

This is a young and growing university, but it has already fulfilled Bishop Hurst's enlightened hope for the study of his-

[2] Theodore C. Sorensen, *Kennedy* (New York: Harper and Row, 1965), pp. 730–733.

[3] Washington *Post*, June 11, 1963.

[4] Sorensen, *Kennedy*, p. 733.

[5] Washington *Post*, June 2, 1964.

[6] Do you think Kennedy's use of humor in his opening sentence is appropriate for winning the attention and goodwill of his audience?

tory and public affairs in a city devoted to the making of history and to the conduct of the public's business.

By sponsoring this institution of higher learning for all who wish to learn, whatever their color or their creed, the Methodists of this area and the nation deserve the nation's thanks. And I commend all those who are today graduating.

Prof. Woodrow Wilson once said that every man sent out from a university should be a man of his nation as well as a man of his time and I'm confident that the men and women who carry the honor of graduating from this institution will continue to give from their lives, from their talents a high measure of public service and public support.

"There are few earthly things more beautiful than a university," wrote John Masefield, in his tribute to English universities—and his words are equally true today. He did not refer to towers or to campus. He admired the splendid beauty of a university, because it was, he said,

> "a place where those who hate ignorance may strive to know, where those who perceive truth may strive to make others see."[7]

I have, therefore, chosen this time and place to discuss a topic on which ignorance too often abounds and the truth is too rarely perceived—and that is the most important topic on earth: peace.

What kind of peace do I mean and what kind of peace do we seek? Not a Pax Americana enforced on the world by American weapons of war. Not the peace of the grave or the security of the slave. I am talking about the genuine peace—the kind of peace that makes life on earth worth living—and the kind that enables men and nations to grow and to hope and build a better life for their children—not merely peace for Americans but peace for all men and women—not merely peace in our time but peace in all time.

I speak of peace because of the new face of war. Total war makes no sense in an age where great powers can maintain large and relatively invulnerable nuclear forces and refuse to

[7] What effect does the citing of Bishop Hurst, President Wilson, and Masefield have on the tone of the speech?

surrender without resort to those forces. It makes no sense in an age when a single nuclear weapon contains almost ten times the explosive force delivered by all the Allied air forces in the second world war. It makes no sense in an age when the deadly poisons produced by a nuclear exchange would be carried by wind and water and soil and seed to the far corners of the globe and to generations yet unborn.

Today the expenditure of billions of dollars every year on weapons acquired for the purpose of making sure we never need them is essential to the keeping of peace. But surely the acquisition of such idle stockpiles—which can only destroy and can never create—is not the only, much less the most efficient, means of assuring peace.[8]

I speak of peace, therefore, as the necessary rational end of rational men. I realize the pursuit of peace is not as dramatic as the pursuit of war—and frequently the words of the pursuer fall on deaf ears. But we have no more urgent task.

Some say that it is useless to speak of peace or world law or world disarmament—and that it will be useless until the leaders of the Soviet Union adopt a more enlightened attitude. I hope they do. I believe we can help them do it.

But I also believe that we must re-examine our own attitudes—as individuals and as a nation—for our attitude is as essential as theirs. And every graduate of this school, every thoughtful citizen who despairs of war and wishes to bring peace, should begin by looking inward—by examining his own attitude towards the course of the cold war and toward freedom and peace here at home.

First: Examine our attitude towards peace itself. Too many of us think it is impossible. Too many think it is unreal. But that is a dangerous defeatist belief. It leads to the conclusion that war is inevitable—that mankind is doomed—that we are gripped by forces we cannot control.

We need not accept that view. Our problems are man-made. Therefore, they can be solved by man. And man can be as big as he wants. No problem of human destiny is beyond human

[8] This paragraph is filled with stylistic devices. How many can you identify and why are they effective?

beings. Man's reason and spirit have often solved the seemingly unsolvable—and we believe they can do it again.[9]

I am not referring to the absolute, infinite concepts of universal peace and goodwill of which some fantasies and fanatics dream. I do not deny the value of hopes and dreams but we merely invite discouragement and incredulity by making that our only and immediate goal.

Let us focus instead on a more practical, more attainable peace—based not on a sudden revolution in human nature but on a gradual evolution in human institutions—on a series of concrete actions and effective agreements which are in the interests of all concerned.

There is no single, simple key to this peace—no grand or magic formula to be adopted by one or two powers. Genuine peace must be the product of many nations, the sum of many acts. It must be dynamic, not static, changing to meet the challenge of each new generation. For peace is a process—a way of solving problems.

With such a peace, there will still be quarrels and conflicting interests, as there are within families and nations. World peace, like community peace, does not require that each man love his neighbor—it requires only that they live together with mutual tolerance, submitting their disputes to a just and peaceful settlement. And history teaches us that enmities between nations, as between individuals, do not last forever. However fixed our likes and dislikes may seem, the tide of time and events will often bring surprising changes in the relations between nations and neighbors.

So let us persevere. Peace need not be impracticable—and war need not be inevitable. By defining our goal more clearly—by making it seem more manageable and less remote—we can help all people to see it, to draw hope from it, and to move irresistibly towards it.

And second: let us re-examine our attitude towards the

[9] Analyze the reasoning in this paragraph. Is Kennedy's conclusion acceptable?

Soviet Union. It is discouraging to think that their leaders may actually believe what their propagandists write.

It is discouraging to read a recent authoritative Soviet text on military strategy and find, on page after page, wholly baseless and incredible claims—such as the allegation that

> "American imperialists circles are preparing to unleash different types of war . . . that there is a very real threat of a preventative war being unleashed by American imperialists against the Soviet Union . . . (and that) the political aims,"

and I quote,

> "of the American imperialists are to enslave economically and politically the European and other capitalist countries . . . (and) to achieve world domination . . . by means of aggressive war."

Truly, as it was written long ago: "The wicked flee when no man pursueth." Yet it is sad to read these Soviet statements—to realize the extent of the gulf between us. But it is also a warning—a warning to the American people not to fall into the same trap as the Soviets, not to see only a distorted and desperate view of the other side, not to see conflict as inevitable, accommodation as impossible and communication as nothing more than an exchange of threats.

No government or social system is so evil that its people must be considered as lacking in virtue. As Americans, we find Communism profoundly repugnant as a negation of personal freedom and dignity. But we can still hail the Russian people for their many achievements—in science and space, in economic and industrial growth, in culture, in acts of courage.

Among the many traits the peoples of our two countries have in common, none is stronger than our mutual abhorrence of war. Almost unique among the major world powers, we have never been at war with each other. And no nation in the history of battle ever suffered more than the Soviet Union in the second world war. At least 20,000,000 lost their lives. Countless millions of homes and families were burned or sacked. A third of the nation's territory, including two-thirds of its industrial base, was turned into a wasteland—a loss equivalent to the destruction of this country east of Chicago.[10]

Today, should total war ever break out again—no matter how—our two countries will be the primary targets. It is an ironic but accurate fact that the two strongest powers are the two in the most danger of devastation. All we have built, all we have worked for, would be destroyed in the first 24 hours. And even in the cold war—which brings burdens and dangers to so many countries, including this nation's closest allies—our two countries bear the heaviest burdens. For we are both devoting massive sums of money to weapons that could be better devoted to combat ignorance, poverty and disease.

We are both caught up in a vicious and dangerous cycle with suspicion on one side breeding suspicion on the other, and new weapons begetting counter-weapons.

In short, both the United States and its allies, and the Soviet Union and its allies, have a mutually deep interest in a just and genuine peace and in halting the arms race. Agreements to this end are in the interests of the Soviet Union as well as ours—and even the most hostile nations can be relied upon to accept and keep those treaty obligations and only those treaty obligations, which are in their own interest.

So, let us not be blind to our differences—but let us also direct attention to our common interests and the means by which those differences can be resolved. And if we cannot end now our differences, at least we can help make the world safe for diversity. For, in the final analysis, our most basic common link is that we all inhabit this small planet. We all breathe the same air. We all cherish our children's future. And we are all mortal.[11]

Third: Let us re-examine our attitude towards the cold war, remembering we are not engaged in a debate, seeking to pile up debating points.

We are not here distributing blame or pointing the finger of judgment. We must deal with the world as it is, and not as it

[10] What method does Kennedy use to make Russian losses more vivid for his American audience?

[11] Classify the appeals in this paragraph. Are they effective?

might have been had the history of the last eighteen years been different.

We must, therefore, persevere in the search for peace in the hope that constructive changes within the Communist bloc might bring within reach solutions which now seem beyond us. We must conduct our affairs in such a way that it becomes in the Communists' interest to agree on a genuine peace. And above all, while defending our own vital interests, nuclear powers must avert those confrontations which bring an adversary to a choice of either a humiliating retreat or a nuclear war. To adopt that kind of course in the nuclear age would be evidence only of the bankruptcy of our policy—or of a collective death-wish for the world.

To secure these ends, America's weapons are non-provocative, carefully controlled, designed to deter and capable of selective use. Our military forces are committed to peace and disciplined in self-restraint. Our diplomats are instructed to avoid unnecessary irritants and purely rhetorical hostility.

For we can seek a relaxation of tensions without relaxing our guard. And, for our part, we do not need to use threats to prove that we are resolute. We do not need to jam foreign broadcasts out of fear our faith will be eroded. We are unwilling to impose our system on any unwilling people—but we are willing and able to engage in peaceful competition with any people on earth.[12]

Meanwhile, we seek to strengthen the United Nations, to help solve its financial problems, to make it a more effective instrument for peace, to develop it into a genuine world security system—a system capable of resolving disputes on the basis of law, of insuring the security of the large and the small, and of creating conditions under which arms can finally be abolished.

At the same time we seek to keep peace inside the non-Communist world, where many nations, all of them our friends, are divided over issues which weaken Western unity which invite Communist intervention or which threaten to erupt into war.

[12] The President is obviously chastizing the Soviet government. Why does he use indirect statement when making the charges?

Our efforts in West New Guinea, in the Congo, in the Middle East and the Indian subcontinent have been persistent and patient despite criticism from both sides. We have also tried to set an example for others—by seeking to adjust small but significant differences with our own closest neighbors in Mexico and Canada.

Speaking of other nations, I wish to make one point clear. We are bound to many nations by alliances. These alliances exist because our concern and theirs substantially overlap. Our commitment to defend Western Europe and West Berlin, for example, stands undiminished because of the identity of our vital interests. The United States will make no deal with the Soviet Union at the expense of other nations and other peoples, not merely because they are our partners, but also because their interests and ours converge.

Our interests converge, however, not only in defending the frontiers of freedom, but in pursuing the paths of peace.

It is our hope—and the purpose of allied policies—to convince the Soviet Union that she, too, should let each nation choose its own future, so long as that choice does not interfere with the choices of others. The Communist drive to impose their political and economic system on others is the primary cause of world tension today. For there can be no doubt that, if all nations could refrain from interfering in the self-determination of others, the peace would be much more assured.

This will require a new effort to achieve world law—a new context for world discussions. It will require increased understanding between the Soviets and ourselves. And increased understanding will require increased contact and communication.

One step in this direction is the proposed arrangement for a direct line between Moscow and Washington, to avoid on each side the dangerous delays, misunderstanding, and misreadings of the other's actions which might occur in a time of crisis.

We have also been talking in Geneva about other first-step measures of arms control, designed to limit the intensity of the arms race and reduce the risks of accidental war.

Our primary long-range interest in Geneva, however, is general and complete disarmament—designed to take place by stages, permitting parallel political developments to build the new institutions of peace which would take the place of arms. The pursuit of disarmament has been an effort of this Government since the 1920's. It has been urgently sought by the past three Administrations. And however dim the prospects are today, we intend to continue this effort—to continue it in order that all countries, including our own, can better grasp what the problems and the possibilities of disarmament are.

The only major area of these negotiations where the end is in sight—yet where a fresh start is badly needed—is in a treaty to outlaw nuclear tests. The conclusion of such a treaty—so near and yet so far—would check the spiraling arms race in one of its most dangerous areas. It would place the nuclear powers in a position to deal more effectively with one of the greatest hazards which man faces in 1963—the further spread of nuclear weapons. It would increase our security—it would decrease the prospects of war.

Surely this goal is sufficiently important to require our steady pursuit, yielding neither to the temptation to give up the whole effort nor the temptation to give up our insistence on vital and responsible safeguards.

I am taking this opportunity, therefore, to announce two important decisions in this regard:

First: Chairman Khrushchev, Prime Minister Macmillan and I have agreed that high-level discussions will shortly begin in Moscow towards early agreement on a comprehensive test ban treaty. Our hopes must be tempered with the caution of history—but with our hopes go the hopes of all mankind.

Second: To make clear our good faith and solemn convictions on the matter, I now declare that the United States does not propose to conduct nuclear tests in the atmosphere so long as other states do not do so. We will not be the first to resume. Such a declaration is no substitute for a formal binding treaty—but I hope it will help us achieve one. Nor would such a treaty be a substitute for disarmament—but I hope it will help us achieve it.

Finally, my fellow Americans, let us examine our attitude towards peace and freedom here at home. The quality and spirit of our own society must justify and support our efforts abroad. We must show it in the dedication of our own lives—as many of you who are graduating today will have an opportunity to do, by serving without pay in the Peace Corps abroad or in the proposed National Service Corps here at home.

But wherever we are, we must all, in our daily lives, live up to the age-old faith that peace and freedom walk together. In too many of our cities today, the peace is not secure because freedom is incomplete.

It is the responsibility of the executive branch at all levels of government—local, state and national—to provide and protect that freedom for all of our citizens by all means within our authority. It is the responsibility of the legislative branch at all levels, wherever the authority is not now adequate, to make it adequate. And it is the responsibility of all citizens in all sections of this country to respect the rights of others and respect the law of the land.

All this is not unrelated to world peace. "When a man's ways please the Lord," the scriptures tell us, "he maketh even his enemies to be at peace with him." And is not peace, in the last analysis, basically a matter of human rights—the right to live out our lives without fear of devastation—the right to breathe air as nature provided it—the right of future generations to a healthy existence?

While we proceed to safeguard our national interests, let us also safeguard human interests. And the elimination of war and arms is clearly in the interest of both.

No treaty, however much it may be to the advantage of all, however tightly it may be worded, can provide absolute security against the risks of deception and evasion. But it can—if it is sufficiently effective in its enforcement and it is sufficiently in the interests of its signers—offer far more security and far fewer risks than an unabated, uncontrolled, unpredictable arms race.

The United States, as the world knows, will never start a war. We do not want a war. We do not now expect a war. This generation of Americans has already had enough—more than enough—of war and hate and oppression. We shall be prepared if others wish it. We shall be alert to try to stop it. But we shall also do our part to build a world of peace where the weak are safe and the strong are just.

We are not helpless before that task or hopeless of its success. Confident and unafraid, we labor on—not toward a strategy of annihilation but toward a strategy of peace. Thank you.[13]

CRITICAL ANALYSIS AND PROJECTS

1. Examine Kennedy's method of defining peace. Does he successfully avoid platitudes and set the appropriate tone for the remainder of his speech?
2. This speech was intended primarily to improve Soviet and American relations. How does the President direct his appeals to the commencement audience, his American opponents, and the Soviet Government?
3. Make a list of all the conciliatory statements in the speech and determine which ones would be most helpful in relaxing East-West tensions.
4. The three paragraphs concerning immediate test-ban negotiations and the cessation of United States nuclear tests in the atmosphere appear to have been added long after the original draft of the speech was completed. Are they inserted in the best place to gain acceptance by the audience? Should the remainder of the speech have been focused on these two decisions?
5. A writer for *Christian Century* said the speech "made up in earnestness and honesty what it lacked in rhetorical flourishes." Analyze the structure of the sentences and use of figures of speech to determine if the critic is right.
6. Numerous objections were raised against the President's proposals. Read the speeches in the *Congressional Record,* 88th Cong., 1st Sess., 14562–14563, 16782–16808, 16896–16906, and assess his opponents' arguments.

[13] The conclusion to this speech is unusually brief. Is it appropriate? What might have been included in an expanded conclusion?

SELECTED BIBLIOGRAPHY

1. Barrett, Harold. "John F. Kennedy Before the Greater Houston Ministerial Association," *Central States Speech Journal,* XV (November 1964), 259–266.
2. Golden, James L. "John F. Kennedy and the 'Ghosts,'" *Quarterly Journal of Speech,* LII (December 1966), 348–357.
3. Hilsman, Roger. *To Move a Nation: The Politics of Foreign Policy in the Administration of John F. Kennedy.* Garden City, N.Y.: Doubleday, 1967.
4. Ions, Edmund S. *The Politics of John F. Kennedy.* London: Routledge and K. Paul, 1967.
5. *John Fitzgerald Kennedy, 1917–1963: A Chronological List of References.* Washington, D.C.: U.S. Government Printing Office, 1964.
6. Kraus, Sidney, ed. *The Great Debates.* Bloomington, Ind.: Indiana University Press, 1962.
7. Nevins, Allan, ed. *The Strategy of Peace.* New York: Harper and Row, 1960.
8. Sorensen, Theodore C. *Kennedy.* New York: Harper and Row, 1965.
9. Tanzer, Lester, ed. *The Kennedy Circle.* Washington, D.C.: Luce, 1961.
10. White, Theodore H. *The Making of the President, 1960.* New York: Atheneum Publishers, 1961.
11. Wicker, Tom. "Kennedy as a Public Speakah," *The New York Times Magazine* (February 25, 1962), pp. 14, 70–71.
12. Wolfarth, Donald L. "John F. Kennedy in the Tradition of Inaugural Speeches," *Quarterly Journal of Speech,* XLVII (April 1961), 124–132.

IV

BARRY M. GOLDWATER

Peace Through Strength

Senator Barry Goldwater of Arizona had never been a supporter of the Kennedy administration's foreign policy, so it came as no shock to political observers when he announced in a September 1963, speech that he would vote against the nuclear test-ban treaty. He called this maneuver to end the cold war a "political ambush" and said it would "erode our military strength."[1] An architect of the "get tough" policy with communist nations, Goldwater had first clearly outlined his political philosophy in *The Conscience of a Conservative*,[2] a book which won him a national reputation and sold over three and one-half million copies by 1964.

As early as 1961 an organization had been formed to help Goldwater win the Republican presidential nomination, and on January 3, 1964, the Senator formally announced his candidacy. While campaigning in the New Hampshire primary he frequently attacked the Pentagon's decision to phase out manned bombers and to rely on various missile systems for defense. Senator Goldwater, however, failed to win over the voters of the state and lost the mid-March primary to Henry Cabot Lodge by more than 12,000 votes.

The text of the speech is from a press release copy from the Detroit Economic Club. It is printed by permission of Barry M. Goldwater. The speech was given at the Detroit Economic Club in Detroit, Michigan, on March 25, 1964.

[1] Barry Goldwater, "The Test Ban Treaty," *Vital Speeches of the Day*, XXIX (October 1, 1963), 767–768.

[2] Shepherdsville, Ken.: Victor Publishing Co., 1960. L. Brent Bozell, brother-in-law of William Buckley, actually wrote the book.

At a rally sponsored by the Detroit Economic Club on March 25, 1964, he spoke to an audience of nearly 3,000 on his favorite theme of military preparedness. Although several of Secretary of Defense Robert McNamara's Republican friends were in the audience, Senator Goldwater unleashed a "scathing indictment of the Defense Secretary."[3] This was a major policy speech and represents a theme repeated throughout Goldwater's unsuccessful bid for the presidency.

As anyone can tell from the cast of characters this evening, this is a purely non-political gathering. You'll have to excuse me, however, if politics does enter into my remarks. Whether we like it or not, the great issues of the day *are* political. Our choices are political.

The great issues of whether we will let our enterprise economy work, or whether we will let *our people* work or whether we will go backward to the days of bureaucratic economic controls—*that* issue is political. Whether we are to have a foreign policy that means something to friend and foe alike, or whether we will continue to hop from crisis to crisis—*that* issue is political. Whether we are to have a government of balanced powers, or a new political royalty or centralized power—*that* issue is certainly political. Whether we are to live by law, or whether we are to make our laws in the streets—*that* issue is political. And, sadly enough, the very issue of whether we can assure the security of this nation, and effectively bolster the security . . . of the entire free world—*that* grave issue is clearly political too.[4]

Because of this, I ask you to consider, in your conscience and in your heart, that election day 1964 will also be D-Day 1964—*decision day* as to whether this nation is to keep the peace through strength, or whether it will risk war through

[3] *The New York Times,* March 26, 1964.

[4] Is Goldwater's use of repetition an effective rhetorical technique? Does it appear contrived or overworked?

weakness. There are those who seek to complicate this issue. I seek to simplify it so that it may be understood and not glossed over. Questions of life and death *should* be understood. No concepts need more clarity, more understanding. Double-talk and verbal fog is worse than dishonesty at a time such as this. It could be fatal.

Many of you are deeply concerned with this. Many of you are deeply involved *in* this. From this area comes a great share of the tools with which this nation can keep the peace. But from this area, also, has come the leading advocate, the leading architect of a so-called defense policy which, by the late 1960's and the early 1970's, will have turned the shield of the Republic into a Swiss-cheese wall, full of holes—a policy which will have isolated the power of America behind a Maginot line of illusions; a policy which will encourage our enemies to become bolder, to risk the final, fatal step toward nuclear war; a policy which will turn the profession of arms into a second class craft; a policy which will have so hardened the arteries of our defenses that flexible responses to challenge will be impossible, leaving us with the alternatives only of withdrawal or nuclear holocaust.[5]

The architect of this policy is the present Secretary of Defense: a one-time loser with the Edsel, right here in Michigan; a four-time loser in terms of his trips to Viet-Nam; and an all-time loser if his policies, and the policies of the Administration that supports and applauds him, are not changed in 1964![6]

In simplest terms, the policies of this Administration and the adding machine warriors to which it has entrusted our defenses, add up to unilateral disarmament. This, of course, is a perfect complement to a foreign policy which seeks to curry favor with our enemies even as it alienates our friends. It is the perfect support for a national slogan of "Don't Rock the Boat." It is the perfect sugar-coated pill to tranquilize us into

[5] What is your reaction to the figurative expressions in this paragraph? Is it free from "verbal fog"?

[6] Goldwater again uses repetition to heighten his arguments. Is it more effective here or in the second paragraph?

believing that peace can be kept by coming to terms with Communism rather than by *overcoming* Communism.

What peace there is in the world today is the result of our strength. The conflict that breaks out is the result of our weakness. Wherever and whenever we have moved from strength, we have moved to peace. Wherever we have moved from fear or weakness we have moved closer to war.[7]

On the dark day that Nikita Khrushchev sabotaged the Paris Conference, President Eisenhower's Secretary of Defense, Tom Gates, alerted the Strategic Air Command. We moved from resolution and strength. And Nikita Khrushchev backed down. *He* moved from fear. *He* returned to Moscow, via East Berlin, and warned the Communist world to avoid further provocations, to be patient, in effect—to back down. Again, under President Eisenhower, our first move in the Berlin crisis of 1958–1959 was to move an extra aircraft carrier to the Sixth Fleet as a clear warning to the Communists. Khrushchev cooled down again, far more quickly and with far less cost to us than when Robert McNamara called up the reserves in 1961. That was a chaotic and costly maneuver that did nothing but perpetuate the now permanent crisis in Germany.

When our Marines moved into Lebanon, when we moved our naval and air power in the Formosa Straits, we moved closer to peace, not war. It was when our nerves failed at the Bay of Pigs that we moved closer to war by opening the door for the missile crisis. During the missile crisis, briefly, we moved from strength—and the Communists had to retreat. But since then the balance has been tipping away from us again. Indecision and lack of follow-through have stored up Communism's outpost in our hemisphere and have permitted it to expand its influence. A blockade of Cuba would not risk war. It is the blockade against common sense in this Administration that risks war by letting problems fester rather than resolving them.

But let us be very clear on the crucial point—the national power which has permitted us to move from strength in the

[7] Examine these arguments in light of the evidence in the following paragraphs. Does Goldwater establish his claim that strength brings peace, and weakness, war?

past and which even today *could* permit us to do so, *this power is not perpetual or automatic.* It cannot be maintained at a standstill. There is another side to the power equation; the Communist side. If our power remains at a standstill while their's grows we shall be, in effect, disarming ourselves. And this, I charge, is what we are doing.

If the Communists make a major weapons breakthrough while we sit on our plans, burn our bombers, and permit free world alliances to crumble there can be no peace in the world. Communism would have the tools of nuclear blackmail and would use them. And this mighty nation, mighty no longer, would be ringed by crisis, hemmed in by threats, and pressed closer and closer to the brink of war or surrender.[8]

There are four fatal flaws in our defense posture which foreshadow that grim time. These flaws will not be repaired by the men who created them. They have vested interest in their own mistakes. Let me list the flaws and then elaborate upon them. First, we are building a Maginot line of missiles. Second, we are failing to introduce rapid technological advances, sometimes because of false economy, sometimes because of misguided steps toward disarmament. Third, we are permitting our defense policies to disrupt NATO and our other alliances. Fourth, we are downgrading the armed services, ignoring professional military advice and substituting one-man's bookkeeping technique for national policy.[9]

Let's look at the missiles first. They are fine weapons—when and if they work! The industrial know-how that has gone into them is first class. The men who use them are dedicated and skillful. But the systems themselves are complex almost beyond belief. They are not perfect and they are not perfectly reliable. When I questioned this reliability earlier in the year I was answered with a personal attack that even questioned my patriotism. I was not answered with the cold facts of missile reliability.

[8] What kind of appeal is Goldwater using in this paragraph?

[9] This paragraph is designed to prepare the listener for the major arguments in the remainder of the speech. Why is this important in an oral presentation?

How in the name of common sense can we *fail* to be concerned about this question of reliability when twice this year alone, ICBM's have burned in their silos—when we have never tested a Minuteman, an Atlas or a Titan with all their components in a full scale systems test including the warhead explosion!

How can we fail to be concerned about this question of reliability when we have never tested the hardness of our launch sites, when there are plaguing problems of contamination in the very sensitive fuels of the liquid fuel missiles?

How can we fail to be concerned about this question of reliability when we have not tested the reliability of guidance systems under the impact of electromagnetic pulses emitted by a possible counter-missile nuclear blast?

How can we fail to be concerned when the only answers we have been getting have been personal attacks and when tests are made with special crews and under ideal conditions—and when, even then, we have not scored the sort of reliability one should expect from a weapon system on which, in a few years, will rest our major reliance?[10]

I say that drawing-board perfection is not enough for the defense of the United States! I say that ledger-book juggling is not enough for the defense of the United States. When I talk about missile reliability, I do not talk in terms of ideal conditions, of special crews, of ideal preparations. That is the way some people keep their books. I talk of missiles that must be reliable in the worst of conditions even during or after nuclear attack, with crews that never have fired a complete weapon, and on an instant's notice. Only that sort of reliability impresses the enemy. Only that sort of reliability serves to deter war. Today, by Secretary McNamara's own admission, we seek to compensate for the unknown factors of missile reliability by redundancy of system and targeting, by the brute force techniques of extra missiles for every target—by techniques which obviously can be outmoded by qualitative advances in the

[10] This and the preceding three paragraphs constitute a series of rhetorical questions designed to show the weaknesses in America's defense policy. Evaluate this method of argument.

Soviet—advances that are possible as a result of their past high yield and high altitude experiments.

People often have asked why I risked political suicide to vote against the test ban treaty. This is why! Because I fear the suicide of my country far more than the political fate of *any* individual.[11] The Senate Preparedness Subcommittee has warned in a formal report that "it is prudent to assume that the Soviet Union has acquired a unique and potentially valuable body of data on high yield blast, shock, communications blackout, and radiation and electromagnetic phenomena which is not available to the United States."

Then *who* is being reckless with the peace of the world and the security of this nation? I say that reckless men are those who will not face the facts, who ignore the possibility of the Soviet Union developing counter-measures which will immobilize this Maginot Line of missiles that we are building. I say we *need* the missiles. But I say we need tomorrow's missiles as well as yesterday's. Secretary McNamara gives us no assurance of follow-on missiles. This Administration says that they might be provocative! I say that they might save our lives!

We need more to defend this country and keep the peace. We need a *mixture* of forces, we need flexibility. Again, I do not speak only of yesterday's manned bombers. What of tomorrow's? This Administration declares we won't have *any* after 1970! This Administration has not moved ahead with a single new strategic weapons system, missile *or* manned! The weapons we have today are the great legacy of the Eisenhower years. The deterrent gap we face tomorrow is inevitable if no new weapon systems are introduced.

In this tough and troubled world, man is not obsolete. Manned weapons, guided by man's mind, eyes, hands, and heart are not obsolete. Missiles are an *"either or"* weapon. Manned systems alone provide full flexibility—and, again, who is reckless, the man who wants to put all our eggs in a rigid, doomsday system, or the men who want to retain freedom of action, discretion of maneuver, flexibility of response?

[11] A speaker frequently makes statements to increase the audience's respect for him. Is this such a statement? Can you find other similar statements in the speech?

Even in the vastness of space there may be a mission for man. But space weaponery is taboo to this Administration—despite obvious Soviet interest in it.

Manned systems have many characteristics lacking in ballistic missiles—the ability to hit unanticipated targets, to perform post-attack reconnaissance, to do the jobs of mopping up, to allow margins for the errors of missile targeting, to *permit* maneuver, to be *re-used* and *recalled* if desired. The motto of the Strategic Air Command is "Peace is our Profession." Let us make sure that they have the tools to practice that profession!

The second flaw in our defenses is technological decline. The new A-11 of which President Johnson boasts was started during the Eisenhower years—*not the McNamara years!* The TFX, Mr. McNamara's six-and-a-half billion dollar contribution to campaign politics, is a second best weapons system. As you probably know, by the way, that plane wasn't even called the TFX during the election in Texas—where it is supposed to be built. It was called the LBJ!

Furthermore, Secretary McNamara, the one-man band, reversed the unanimous recommendations of the impartial source selection boards and made the TFX award to the *highest* bidder with *least* advanced design. He rejected as too risky for American skills such advances as thrust reversers to give better control, and the extensive use of titanium to provide a lighter plane for carrier use. I mention those details because the A-11 *does* use titanium and because the Department of Defense is now considering thrust reversers *and* titanium for TFX itself! Again, it seems, the human computers have goofed!

An even more striking case of technological backwardness is the McNamara veto of the nuclear aircraft carrier. It was a Democrat Congressman, Melvin Price, who said that building conventional carriers today is "like the Union Pacific Railroad going back to steam engines because the Diesel costs a little bit more." The full Joint Committee on Atomic Energy, the Department of the Navy, and many others have warned that we must have the most modern carriers. Had Robert McNamara been Secretary in the last century we would never have gone from sail to steam!

Let me remind you that I am not arguing *against* real cost *consciousness.* I *am* arguing against the lack of perspective that is penny-wise and pound-foolish with the future of the entire free world! Today, Secretary McNamara himself has pointed out, some 75 percent of our nuclear capability is carried in the bomb bays of manned aircraft. And he is phasing out *all* of that capacity, while adding only a relatively few missiles, with generally smaller war heads, to replace it. We can, under this plan, easily see the time when our nuclear delivery capability will be cut by anywhere from 25 to 50 percent!

Will this drop in strength soothe the Soviet? Or will it encourage them to take even bolder steps? Who is being reckless with the future of the free world? Those who call for peace through strength? Or those who risk war and defeat through weakness?

And now the third flaw in our defenses, the flaw that marks this Administration as the most isolationist Administration since the head-in-the-sand days that immediately preceded the Second World War. Today we are following the same tactics of disarmament, the same vain hopes of appeasement that *encouraged* the Second World War. Weakness was not the way to peace then and it isn't today. Hitler could have been deterred without war in the Thirties! Khrushchev can be deterred without war in the Sixties.

But, this isolationist defense policy of ours threatens to destroy the NATO alliance today. Secretary McNamara took our missiles out of Italy and Turkey, after the Cuban missile crisis, in a way that made it look for all the world like a deal. He cancelled out Great Britain's bid for nuclear partnership, when he scuttled the skybolt. He has clashed with our NATO commanders over the role of tactical nuclear weapons in Europe. France, for one, apparently *is* convinced that we are retreating into nuclear isolation in an illusory Fortress America. No wonder that Charles de Gaulle is behaving the way he is! He is a Frenchman, thinking of France.

God help us if we can't have American leadership that thinks as forcefully and devoutly of America! That thinks as forcefully of the cause of freedom all over the world and seeks to re-unite the free world, not divide it. The more our defense policies move toward a one-weapon system, toward major reliance on missiles based in the U.S., toward denial of real nuclear partnership with our allies—so long as we move that way, NATO will decline and eventually will fall apart. There may be no NATO after 1970 if the policies of this Administration are permitted to continue.

Is that what Americans want? To be isolated, to be friendless, to be prepared to defend freedom only by the devastation of intercontinental nuclear war? Americans will answer *that* question this November.

And now for the fourth flaw in our defense. I don't care how many computers Mr. McNamara has, or how many "whiz kids" man them, the life-or-death decisions of national defense cannot wisely be made in an atmosphere that supresses dissent, ignores experienced military advice, down-grades military men, and divides the Pentagon into a five-sided arena for the abuse of ideas rather than the development of ideas.

Take just one notable example, the case of the X-22, the VSTOL, vertical take-off and landing aircraft. It involved a twenty million dollar research contract. Seventy-five Navy professionals—civilian and uniformed—spent 4,000 man hours evaluating the designs of two aircraft companies. They made a clear choice, for the best plane at the least cost. The Secretary of the Navy, Fred Korth, excused himself from involvement because he had been a director of the parent company of one of the firms involved.

Next, Secretary McNamara's deputy whiz kid spent less than a half hour conferring with some of his colleagues—but not with any of the military men involved! He didn't even have a briefing on the subject! And in that half hour he reversed 4,000 hours of careful evaluation! Why? Perhaps there is a detail that should be explained. He wanted to get an insight of the management capabilities of the company to whom he arbitrarily awarded the contract. Who did he ask? As you might expect, Secretary Korth, the former board member who, earlier, had disqualified himself. Again, we saw the McNamara team accepting the poorest plane at the highest cost because of its delusions of competence. This amounts to nothing less than contract by crony and weapons by whimsy. It destroys the front of false economy behind which so many errors are being hidden.

Robert McNamara may be the greatest bookkeeper we have ever had in government. He claims to have saved a lot of money. But he has lost more morale in the military than any Secretary of the services we ever have had! The record of defense management has been obscured by the brilliance of news *management*. The overuse of official secrecy has clamped lids on reams of damaging testimony given before Congressional committees.

But the truth is apparent. We have *no new strategic weapons*. We *do* face the disruption of our alliance system. We *are* withdrawing into a Fortress America. Our power *is* at a standstill. Our military morale *is* declining. And Robert McNamara *is* the Secretary of Defense. His ledgersheet *is* leading to a deterrent gap in the next decade. He sees the world in a rear-view mirror. He sees the enemy through rose-colored glasses. He seeks defense through disarmament, but he risks the peace through creeping weakness.

The shield of peace[12] is the power of the peace-loving nations. The day that shield drops is the day that bombs may drop. Today, the preponderant strength we have carried over from the Eisenhower years gives us the capability to rebuff and roll back Communism, and also the power to deter war. Today it is the *will to win* that we lack. Tomorrow, if we do not change our course and our commanders, we may not have the capability even if we *should* find the will!

I do not want to risk the security of this nation, of the entire free world by replacing the real shield of peace with vain hopes and misplaced faith. *This is no computer room game we are playing.*

This is freedom's time on the line of history. And if we cannot or will not defend ourselves it might well be freedom's *last* time for dark centuries to come. Let our arms match our

[12] Evaluate this statement as a metaphor for America's defense system. Is it vivid and appropriate? What metaphors can you suggest to replace it?

cause! Let our men match the times! This is the way to peace through strength. Let our people go *that way!* This is the way freedom's cause can win, *without war,* but with honor and justice. This is the victory that we must seek.

CRITICAL ANALYSIS AND PROJECTS

1. Senator Goldwater argues in this speech and throughout the 1964 campaign that the best guarantee for world peace is American military preparedness. Although he repeatedly said he was for peace, the American public considered him "trigger-happy." What arguments or appeals in this speech might give listeners that impression?
2. Goldwater's speech has a clear pattern of organization. Note especially his method of forecasting what points he intends to cover and then his systematic treatment of each point. Why is this deductive pattern of organization effective when addressing a friendly audience rather than a hostile one?
2\. How does his strategy of blaming Secretary McNamara for all the alleged errors in defense planning affect you? How great is the danger that the audience will feel sympathy for the Secretary of Defense?
4\. What kinds of support material does Goldwater use to substantiate his charges against McNamara?
5\. Are terms like "adding machine warriors," "the one-man band," and "deputy whiz kid" name-calling devices or merely descriptive figures? Interpret Goldwater's use of them.
6\. Goldwater seems to equate disarmament with "creeping weakness." Phrase a resolution on this topic and have three other members of the class join you in a debate.
7\. Organize a group discussion to assess the problems of arms control. See items 4. and 5. in the bibliography for basic readings.

SELECTED BIBLIOGRAPHY

1. Bell, Jack. *Mr. Conservative: Barry Goldwater*. Garden City, N.Y.: Doubleday, 1962.
2. Boller, Paul F. *Quotemanship*. Dallas: Southern Methodist University Press, 1967.

3. Brooks, William D. "A Field Study of the Johnson and Goldwater Campaign Speeches in Pittsburgh," *Southern Speech Journal,* XXXII (Summer 1967), 273–281.
4. Davis, Jerome, ed. *Disarmament: A World View.* New York: The Citadel Press, 1964.
5. Dougherty, James E., and J. F. Lehman, Jr. *Arms Control for the Late Sixties.* Toronto, Canada: D. Van Nostrand Co., 1967.
6. Goldwater, Barry M. *Where I Stand.* New York: McGraw-Hill, 1962.
7. ———. *Why Not Victory?* New York: McGraw-Hill, 1962.
8. Hess, Karl. *In a Cause That Will Triumph.* Garden City, N.Y.: Doubleday, 1967.
9. Lokos, Lionel. *Hysteria 1964: The Fear Campaign Against Barry Goldwater.* New Rochelle, N.Y.: Arlington House, 1967.
10. McNamara, Robert S. "Remarks Before the Economic Club of New York," in *American Military Thought,* Walter Millis, ed. (Indianapolis: Bobbs-Merrill, 1966).
11. Rovere, Richard. "The Minds of Barry Goldwater," *Harper's Magazine,* CCXXIX (September 1964), 37–42.
12. Strausz-Hupe, Robert, William R. Kintner, and Stefan T. Possony. *A Forward Strategy for America.* New York: Harper and Brothers, 1961.
13. Voss, Earl H. *Nuclear Ambush: The Test-Ban Trap.* Chicago: Henry Regnery Co., 1963.
14. Wrage, Ernest J. "The Little World of Barry Goldwater," *Western Speech,* XXVII (Fall 1963), 207–215.

PART THREE

RELIGION AND WAR

V

JAMES E. DOUGHERTY

Arms and the Western Conscience

Churchmen have long pondered the proper position of religion toward the conduct of human conflict. The positions have ranged from holy war to just war to pacificism. Nuclear weapons—and especially the policy of nuclear deterrence, with American and Russian missiles aimed at each other's cities—have caused widespread debate among clergymen and laymen in the United States about the morality of Western defense policy. Professor James E. Dougherty, a Catholic layman, has specialized in the problems of arms control since 1959 and has written frequently on morality and the strategy of deterrence.

Dougherty is professor of politics at Saint Joseph's College in Philadelphia and an associate of the Foreign Policy Research Institute of the University of Pennsylvania. In 1964 he served for one year as professor of political affairs at the National War College in Washington, D.C. He has co-authored four books on arms control, including *Morality and Modern Warfare* and *Arms Control for the Late Sixties.*[1]

He disapproves of unilateral disarmament and argues that man will have to live with his new discoveries about the

Reprinted from *Congressional Record*, 88th Cong., 2nd Sess. (June 3, 1964), pp. 12567–12568, by permission of Dr. James E. Dougherty, Professor of Politics, St. Joseph's College, Philadelphia; Associate of the Foreign Policy Research Institute, University of Pennsylvania.

[1] New York: Helicon, 1960; Princeton: Van Nostrand, 1967.

atomic universe for a long time.[2] While he recognizes the right of every individual to determine his own position on war, he urges Christians to reject nuclear pacifism. Furthermore, he says, "the individual Christian, although he may abjure reliance on force where his own welfare is concerned . . . cannot deny the obligations of the State to protect the common good by the threat or use of force when necessary."[3]

On June 2, 1964, Dougherty delivered the speech included here at a Washington dinner of the Catholic Association for International Peace in honor of Father Edward A. Conway, S.J., director of the Center for Peace Research at Creighton University. After discussing the reasoning of pacifists, Dougherty rejects their claim that they represent the true spirit of Christianity in the 1960s and argues that a nuclear deterrence policy is not antithetic to Christian morality. He concludes with an appeal for cooperation between pacifists and defense strategists in determining how to preserve freedom in the world.

We are all in agreement that the arms problem which weighs so heavily upon modern man is a profoundly spiritual one. In every age, the specter of war has prompted poets to ponder what man has made of man. All the great religious teachers have warned against the lust for power. Philosophers have cautioned rulers to be slow to resort to force, lest man become indistinguishable from the savage beast. Countless writers have condemned certain modes of warfare as being immoral, illegal, or uncivilized. Prophets have held forth visions of a day when swords would be beaten into ploughshares and men would no longer be given to war.

To delve into the issues of war and peace, we can perhaps select no better point of departure than that of the Western conscience. This conscience has been a mighty force in history.

[2] James E. Dougherty, "The Christian and Nuclear Pacifism," *The Catholic World*, CXCVIII (March 1964), 345.

[3] *Ibid.*, p. 339.

It is still a uniquely sensitive instrument for analyzing the affairs of governments. This does not mean that Western civilization alone has produced a sense of public morality regarding the use of force by states. In other great civilizations, the leading ethical teachers have counseled against an excessive reliance upon arms, and some of them have preached a doctrine of nonviolence and harmlessness toward all living things. In fact, India's Gandhian tradition has had some impact upon the development of pacifist thought in the West. Nevertheless, I would suggest that the disarmament and peace movements of our day draw their inspiration mainly from a form of idealism which is distinctive to Western culture.

The nuclear pacifist[4] is quite right to insist that the issues of defense policy involve moral questions of the utmost gravity. In this respect, he serves the society better than the technocrat who cannot be bothered with morality. But the pacifist is wrong if he assigns to himself a monopoly of virtue—if he thinks that his own approach to the problems of nuclear weapons constitutes the only authentic moral response. Some of our policymakers seem ill at ease when moral questions are raised. They suspect vaguely that any attempt to examine the arms problem from a moral point of view might strengthen the case for or the cause of unilateral disarmament, or else push our country toward complete disarmament too fast and at almost any cost in concessions to the Soviets. But sound moral analysis need not put the United States at any military, strategic, or political disadvantage. Morality is the application of the highest reason, and reason does not play tragic tricks upon its practitioners. If some people fear that moral analysis does entail disadvantages, this unfortunate impression must perhaps be attributed to the fact that extremists in the peace movement have often equated the so-called moral approach with all sorts of irresponsible proposals.

There are many good but naive people in the peace movement who believe that the last best hope of earth is the willingness of men to picket the White House or to march to

[4] **Why does Dougherty say "nuclear pacifist" instead of just "pacifist"?**

Aldermaston. They proclaim in effect that all advocates of rapid disarmament stand among the elect, in contrast to the misguided or malicious proponents of defense policies. Only the propagandist wishes that the lines between good and evil could be drawn so simply. For pacifists to look upon all supporters of a nuclear defense policy as potential Dr. Strangeloves is no more justified than for the advocates of deterrence to brand all demonstrators for total disarmament as Communist sympathizers.[5]

Not all the marchers for total disarmament are necessarily moral in their motivations. The peace movement derives at least some of its strength not from any altruistic ideals but from the sheer desire for biological survival. No one can deny that the preservation of the human species is a fundamental moral imperative. All other moral efforts presuppose this. But moral values themselves must arise from something spiritually deeper than the brooding fear of self-extinction. Fear should be the beginning, not the end, of wisdom. Any man who is more anxious to prolong his own existence than to uphold the quality of human life itself will hardly make a sacrifice for any cause, however noble. The crass epicurean will purchase his physical safety and comfort at the expense of all those values which fall below the threshold of his own survival.

It would be grossly unfair to suggest that most pacifists belong to this school. The true pacifist is opposed to the use of force precisely because he is interested in values and in the quality of human life. He detests the notion of nuclear violence, and this does not mean that he is indifferent to freedom and justice. He believes firmly that the moral order cannot, in the final analysis, be safeguarded by physical force. The genuine pacifist fears that a nation which rests its security upon the massive deterrent of nuclear power unconsciously undermines the moral quality of its own life. At his finest, the pacifist is not preoccupied with self-existence. He is moved by a concern over the preservation of civilized life on this planet (as every intelligent man must be) . Beyond this, he testifies to

[5] What special insights does this statement give the listener about Dougherty's personal beliefs?

a spiritual concept of man which transcends the notion that right needs might. When he meets a Christian who supports the policy of nuclear deterrence, the pacifist chides him for being caught in a basic self-deception—for threatening to do something in retaliation which cannot morally be done, while hoping that he shall never have to carry out his threat.

For many years, the barbs of the pacifists have been piercing my thick spiritual hide. Nevertheless, after much soul-searching, I cannot accept the pacifist position.[6] In my reading of the relationship between the Old Testament and the New, between the person and the State, between the natural and the supernatural, and between the orders of justice and charity, it does not seem that the maintenance of a nuclear deterrent is intrinsically immoral, or that the law of force has been historically abrogated by the law of love. Not he alone is Christian who despises all instruments of power as evil, who shuns modern weapons technology and washes his hands of it and flees from it as though it were the work of the devil. Some Christians recognize that massive power exists and must be managed. The mere existence of these modern weapons is tragic but not immoral; we often confuse the two. Morality is determined by purpose and intention.[7] How and to what ends shall we use this power in our hands? These are moral questions. The pacifist says that they will surely come to no good and hence must be renounced. My answer is that we hope they will be productive of good and that the worst thing to do in the present historical context is to downgrade the deterrent by embracing a lopsided, unilateral pacifism. So long as nuclear force can be used as an instrument of terror and injustice, the same kind of force must be retained as a deterrent tool of justice.

I realize that States always appeal to the justice of their policies as the figleaf of their moral respectability. But this fact fails to prove that there is no such thing as justice in the world. Some Christian pacifists argue that when all the cor-

[6] How is this statement supposed to affect the listeners?

[7] Does Dougherty's audience have to accept this premise before it can accept the remainder of his arguments?

rupt and immortal tendencies in modern Western culture have been taken into account, our civilization turns out to be no better than any other, not even a totalitarian one. The Christian must always remember the beam in his own eye. He cannot deny that, East and West, we have all gone astray together. All men in all social systems stand equally in need of redemption. Yet when he has made his mea culpa, he must still strive for an objective view of the international situation. When I do this, I am convinced that the political principles, the social values, the spiritual ideals and even most of the institutions of the Western liberal civilization are superior to those of the Communist system, and are worth defending with force.

Western culture has given to the world modern science, the modern democratic state, and the idea of a refined humanity. Indeed, what is best in Marxist socialism is the fruit of Western culture, with its Jewish and Christian, its Greek and Roman, and its European, content. The idea of independence which has burned in the breasts of Asians and Africans, spurring them on in the postwar period to throw off the yoke of Western imperialism, can be traced to no other source than Western education. Never in history has there been such a smooth transition from colonialism to independence. The process succeeded largely because Western elites were basically sympathetic with the movement. The Western nations have done by far the most to promote the economic and social development of the emerging countries, and will continue to do so. On the whole, the record of the West in the recent past is one that the West can be proud of, instead of indulging in unprofitable self-recrimination over the sins of the more remote past. Finally, the vision of an international family of free states united in a pluralist community, living and letting live, working out their problems peacefully and decently, is a distinctive product of Western liberal thought. If the United Nations is someday to be what its architects dreamed of, then the ideals of the West must remain a dynamic, creative force in world history; whatever synthesis of social systems may ultimately emerge, it must embody more respect for the free person than adulation of total social control. The West still has a great deal to offer the world, and a great deal to do for the world. It is by no means a perfect society, but it renews itself by engaging in constant moral self-evaluation. Its peoples measure the policies of their governments against ethical standards more so than in any other region of the world. If the West should ever go under, mankind would be incomparably poorer; the loss would be incalculable.

This is why I reject the contention that pacifism is the acid test of Christianity in the 1960's. The Western nations are entitled to maintain a nuclear deterrent against an adversary who is likely to be impressed by that power. We would do well to remember, as Max Lerner has pointed out, that we really face two great dangers, not one: "There is the danger that the world will become a mound of radiated ashes, and there is also the danger that it will become an ant colony, under a commanding elite that . . . does not hesitate to use the conscience of atomic man for its own power purposes." Both of these represent high moral challenges to our ingenuity. We shall fail if we worry about only one of them. America must wield its vast power responsibly and shrewdly to influence the course of events in two directions–toward a more stable peace and toward the greater freedom of the human spirit.

Most pacifists are offended by the suggestion that the policy of responsible deterrence has succeeded in discouraging at least overt aggression. Deterrence alone, of course, does not solve all our problems. We need much more in the nonmilitary sector. We most certainly should increase our efforts–doubling or tripling them in the next 10 years–to help the peoples of the developing countries create the conditions for the production of social wealth. We are not afraid of engaging the Soviets on the field of peaceful competition. In fact, we are happy to do so. But if the international strategic contest is being lifted to a higher, more constructive plane, this is not because the Communists disdain military power; it is because they respect it. The superiority of the American deterrent is the indispensable condition of peaceful competition, until effective solutions to the arms problem can be reached.[8]

[8] Why is the audience likely to accept this statement, although Dougherty offers little evidence or reasoning to support it?

We should not fail to explore any opportunities which may open up for meaningful arms agreements with the Soviets—agreements which will enhance the safety of the international environment. At the same time, we should remain on our guard against unwarranted optimism. The world is changing rapidly in many respects. But not everything changes. Certain features of the cold war are more persistent than some of us like to think. A system which for four decades has institutionalized the techniques of conflict and expansion can hardly be expected to shift course suddenly. Catholics are sometimes accused of adhering rigidly to the thesis that communism cannot change. This is a most inaccurate interpretation of the Catholic attitude (if one can speak of such a thing). In history, everything changes except the inner essence of Christianity and of the church. No one can rule out the possibility that Soviet communism may evolve in a more benign direction. But after only 1 year or so of ambiguous detente, it is premature to declare that the Soviets are permanently mellowing in their foreign policy. More than once in the past we have learned to our regret that one swallow does not make a spring. Although the Soviets are encountering economic difficulties at home and political squabbles within their state system, there is no evidence that their foreign policy is suffering setbacks in southeast Asia, in Egypt, in India, in Cyprus, and in other areas of the globe. When we assess the current phase of Soviet-American relations, we should not let the wish be father to the thought.[9]

To secure the peace, it is not enough to describe the horrors of war. Since the clear pronouncements of Pope Pius XII, Catholic theologians will not defend a strategy which intends the wholesale obliteration of cities. But neither will the church condemn nuclear weapons and nuclear deterrence as intrinsically immoral. Pope John XXIII refused to do this in Pacem in Terris. He warned that nations cannot always depend for peace upon a mechanistic balancing of forces, and that nations must seek to base their relations on mutual trust.

[9] Is this the best way to warn listeners against letting their desires distort reality?

He added, however, that no nation can be expected to subscribe to an arms reduction plan which involves placing itself at an unfair disadvantage. The late Holy Father said that arms reduction must be reciprocal and subject to effective control. This is what the long years of negotiations have been all about.

On the disarmament front, the prospects for general and complete disarmament are now being looked at more soberly than was the case a few years ago—on both sides—and practical partial measures are under discussion again. The Soviets are still sensitive on the subject of international inspection; their position has not changed noticeably in recent years. There are still some fundamental technical and political problems which have not been solved: I am thinking of the question of hidden stockpiles out of previous production; Soviet reluctance to strengthen the peacekeeping machinery of the United Nations; and the problems posed by France and China. If the Soviets are as worried about China as they sometimes appear to be, they might be unable to contemplate seriously any actual destruction of weapons. The Soviets would probably be content to live in a bipolar nuclear world for a while if they could be reasonably sure that it would not become intolerably multipolar. In my estimation, they are not terrified by us. Cuba taught them many lessons. One was that the United States is capable of carefully defining its irreducible national interest—tardily but carefully. The other is that the United States is capable of acting with consummate restraint; it does not pursue strategic advantages ruthlessly.

The arms problem, as you all know, is almost a bottomless pit in its complexity. The most lurid description of the effects of an H-bomb blast, the most caustic critique of the size of our stockpiles, will not serve to lead us out of our impasse. It does us no good to wring our hands and lament that there is so little time. If we have only a little time, then we are in bad shape, because we are going to need a long time. We have been moving into our present predicament for a long time, for several decades; we cannot untangle ourselves as easily as some pacifists believe, through a sudden moral conversion of governments. We are trying to grapple, all at once, with the nature of modern technology, with the structure of the Nation-State system, with very real philosophical differences, and with the orneriness of men. The task confronting us demands a penetrating intelligence uncommon in history—such an intelligence as cannot be hurried by the manipulations of propagandists. In this era of nuclear-tipped missiles, it can be most dangerous to think in terms of readily perceived panaceas to the enduring dilemmas of world politics.

Man has divined the secrets of the atomic universe. He cannot erase from his mind this awful knowledge by any form of political or scientific exorcism, but must live with it for the rest of time. The best he can hope to do is manage this power with wisdom until it can be organized under the world public authority for which Pope John XXIII called. This will require a much greater consensus of values with respect to the nature of the social and moral universe which is man's habitat. It may well be that the two superpowers both wish to avert nuclear war. This is more of a coincident negative interest than a common positive purpose. We have a long way to go to work out, in a spirit of genuine mutuality, a common vision of the kind of international order to which we wish to belong. The effort to do this has been missing through many years of debate. Instead of focusing almost exclusively upon the technical aspects of the arms problem, the United States should challenge the Soviets to enter upon a broader, nonpolemic discussion with us about man: a true political, philosophical, and theological dialog about the relation of past and future, of person and collective, of heaven and earth, of justice and injustice, and the many other questions which divide us to the depths of our souls.

In closing, I would urge that the partisans of peace and the fighters for freedom reopen their lines of communication. The peace movement still has a lot of homework to do on political, technological, and strategic matters. The strategists for defense can stand to turn away occasionally from the cold calculus of deterrence and meditate upon the grave moral and human issues confronting man. Both groups can help each other to arrive at a deeper understanding of reality. Both groups should recognize the dangers of the intellectual schism which has appeared in our country in recent years between the advocates of peace and the advocates of freedom. If we remain divided, the cause of neither peace nor freedom will be served well.[10] The will to peace is not the will to surrender; the will to freedom is not the will to holocaust. This, I take it, is the message which the man whom we honor tonight has been striving these many years to get through to us.

CRITICAL ANALYSIS AND PROJECTS

1. Dougherty defines morality as the "application of the highest reason" and suggests that it is determined by "purpose and intention." What is your definition? Does your definition make the maintenance of a nuclear deterrent immoral?
2. Is Dougherty's major purpose to attack pacifism or to defend a nuclear defense policy? How many kinds of pacifism does he mention?
3. If you were a pacifist listening to Dougherty's speech, which passage would you cite to show his attitude toward your beliefs?
4. How many maxims does Dougherty use to support his case for nuclear deterrence? Are they a valid method of argument?
5. What internal evidence is there that Dougherty has spent much time studying the questions discussed in the speech?
6. Write an essay comparing and contrasting Dougherty's attitude toward American defense policy with John C. Bennett's attitude as expressed in the next speech.
7. Prepare a speech describing and evaluating the nonviolent doctrines of Martin Luther King, Jr., A. J. Muste, or Mohandas Gandhi.

SELECTED BIBLIOGRAPHY

1. Cox, Donald W. *The Perils of Peace.* Philadelphia: Chilton Books, 1965.
2. Dougherty, James E. "Morality and Strategy of Deterrence," *Catholic World,* CXCIV (March 1962), 337–344.

[10] Dougherty calls for a reconciliation between members of the peace movement and defense strategists. Has he chosen a good strategy for bringing them together?

3. ———. "Nuclear Weapons Control," *Current History,* XLVII (July 1964), 31–38.
4. ———. "Catholic Church, War and Nuclear Weapons," *Orbis,* IX (Winter 1966), 845–897.
5. ———, and J. F. Lehman, Jr., eds. *Arms Control for the Late Sixties.* Toronto, Canada: D. Van Nostrand Co., 1967.
6. Lawler, Justus G. *Nuclear War: The Ethic, the Rhetoric, the Reality.* Westminster, Md.: The Newman Press, 1965.
7. Mayer, Peter, ed. *The Pacifist Conscience.* New York: Holt, Rinehart and Winston, 1966.
8. Ramsey, Paul. *War and the Christian Conscience.* Durham, N.C.: Duke University Press, 1961.
9. Russell, Bertrand. *Has Man a Future?* London: George Allen and Unwin Ltd., 1961.
10. Stein, Walter, ed. *Peace on Earth: The Way Ahead.* London: Sheed and Ward, 1966.
11. *We Accuse* [speeches delivered at a "Vietnam Day" protest rally in Berkeley, California]. Berkeley and San Francisco: Diablo Press, 1965.

VI

JOHN C. BENNETT

The Issues of Peace: The Voice of Religion

For more than three years a group of devoted churchmen representing all major religious groups in the United States planned the National Inter-Religious Conference on Peace which was held in Washington, D.C. on March 15–17, 1966. The conference was attended by almost five hundred clergymen and laymen. It received personal letters of best wishes from Secretary General U Thant and President Lyndon Johnson and concluded its deliberations by urging all religious, interreligious, and community groups to intensify their efforts for peace.[1] The use of the mass media greatly heightened the impact of the conference: daily newspaper stories reviewed the major speakers, the national Episcopal radio office taped all the speeches and broadcast an edited program, and the American Broadcasting Company presented a television special on the conference.[2] This was the setting for the Reverend Dr. John C. Bennett, president of Union Theological Seminary, when he presented the keynote address on March 15.

Dr. Bennett is widely known for his leadership in ecumenical movements and his position that religious leaders

Reprinted by permission from a text furnished by John C. Bennett of his speech delivered in Washington, D.C., March 15, 1966.

[1] Homer A. Jack, ed., *Religion and Peace* (Indianapolis: Bobbs-Merrill, 1966) , p. ix.

[2] *Ibid.,* p. xiv. See, for example, the report on the conference in the Washington *Post,* March 16, 1966.

have a responsibility to speak on questions of foreign policy. His beliefs are cogently presented in three of his books: *Christian Ethics and Social Policy* (1946), *Christians and the State* (1958), and *Foreign Policy in Christian Perspective* (1966).[3]

In his address to the conference Dr. Bennett examines six areas in which persons with "religious perspectives and moral sensitivity" have a duty to speak and concludes with an analysis of how the American perception of communism affects foreign policy.

A conference on religion and peace should begin with some affirmations about the basis that our churches and synagogues have for speaking and acting in the sphere of international relations.

Underlying all else that we may say or do here is the Biblical faith that God is Lord of our nation and of all nations. As the prophet said: "All the nations are as nothing before him, they are accounted by him as less than nothing and emptiness." (Isaiah 40:17). As Amos said much earlier: "Did I not bring up Israel from the land of Egypt, and the Philistines from Caphtor and the Syrians from Kir?" (Amos 9:7). The faith that all nations are under the judgment and providence and mercy of God is central to Biblical religion. Since it is the nation that so easily becomes the ultimate object of loyalty for its citizens, this faith in God as transcending the nation is always a warning against national idolatry. And in our time it is political idolatry, the worship of any social group or system, that is the greatest obstacle to the tolerance and humaneness which are essential conditions for decent relations among nations, essential conditions for peace. The form that idolatry takes with people of some sophistication is not so much the explicit worship of the nation as it is the

[3] All three works were published by Charles Scribner's Sons, New York.

assumption that God is always on the side of one's nation, an easy assumption when our adversaries are atheists!

A second basis for all that we say or do may be ultimately derived from Biblical faith but fortunately many people are able to see the truth of it and to be claimed by it for their own lives without awareness of its religious background. I refer to the moral imperatives that, when translated into a social ethic that is relevant to public life, call us to care for the welfare and dignity of all neighbors including enemies, to seek for them justice and freedom. When I speak of justice, I mean a transforming justice that continually raises the level of life of those who have been at a disadvantage. Most of our neighbors in the world at large are victims of poverty and hunger. Only a revolutionary justice can help them. I am not suggesting that there are some religious shortcuts to the proper balance in our world of justice and freedom, both of which depend upon some kind of political order. But our religious imperatives do press upon us to seek these values. Our churches and synagogues should continually disturb us and press us to do what is in our power to deliver God's people everywhere from poverty and hunger, from humiliation and oppression, from anarchy and war. This is all so obvious that I hesitate even to say it and yet these responsibilities are our agenda.

Our problems begin when at a given time we find the quest of one value such as freedom interfering with another such as order or justice. There will be some differences of opinion about this, but I believe that a conference on peace should begin by recognizing that peace is not the only good, that at times it may have to be sacrificed for the sake of other goods.[4] And yet we may still say that total war would probably destroy all the goods for which we strive and that the burden of proof upon those who defend even limited wars must be a heavy one, for limited wars may escalate into total war and nations, including our own, have a habit of assuming too uncritically the moral and political efficacy of military solutions.

I shall add to these bases for what we may do here one more: a realistic understanding of the temptations to which

[4] Do you think Bennett needed to include this reservation?

nations are especially vulnerable. Reinhold Niebuhr has a chapter in his *Moral Man and Immoral Society* on "The Morality of Nations."[5] This is a classic statement of the situation. Let me mention two of his chief emphases: The first is that "patriotism transmutes individual selfishness into national egoism." This enables good men to become the instruments of the pride and ambition and greed of nations. Second he emphasizes the tendency of nations, including the United States, to clothe the national will with idealistic pretensions. He says that "perhaps the most significant moral characteristic of a nation is hypocrisy." This is a hard saying but I recommend this chapter as devotional reading to all the speech writers in this city.

Professor Herbert Butterfield emphasizes the way in which democracies especially become victims of their own frenzied national self-righteousness. He makes much of the idea that the most furious and cruel conflicts are between what he calls "giant organized systems of self-righteousness—each system only delighted to find that the other is wicked—each only too glad that the sins give it the pretext for still deeper hatred and animosity." (*Christianity, Diplomacy and War.*) This is a fairly accurate description of the relations between the United States and China.

George Kennan reminds us of our own national frenzy in the First World War when our enemy was the Germany of Kaiser Wilhelm II, a moderate compared with subsequent adversaries. Kennan says: "There is, let me assure you, nothing more egocentrical than the embattled democracy. It soon becomes the victim of its own propaganda. It then tends to add to its own cause an absolute value which distorts its own vision of everything else. *Its* enemy becomes the embodiment of all evil. *Its* own side, on the other hand, is the center of all virtue." (*Russia and the West.*)

I speak of these tendencies of nations because it behooves us to remember them when we are in church or synagogue. National self-examination and national repentance are difficult

[5] What status does Niebuhr have with Bennett's audience? What is the value of the quotation?

though not impossible. But citizens, each with his own background of faith and commitment, can and do repent in behalf of their nations. A national repentance usually depends upon events, often catastrophic events, which convince men of ordinary prudence that the nation has been following a wrong road. One of the responsibilities of churches and synagogues is to interpret such events.

Let me at once put in a corrective for what I have said. It would be a great error to derive from such a statement about the temptations of nations what we should therefore say "a plague on all houses" and hold ourselves aloof in personal self-righteousness from all of the strivings of our government. We may be tempted to become personally self-righteous because of our criticism of national self-righteousness. Nations at the present time are the only units of power that can do many things that need to be done. Nations have responsibilities that are commensurate with their power. National ideals are not necessarily mere rationalizations of crude national interests. Also what is in the real national interest of the citizens of a nation has its proper claims so long as it is not dressed up with idealism and ideology and made into an absolute. Whatever the errors and self-deceptions of the United States, our country was not wrong about the threat of Hitlerism to humanity and it was not wrong about the need to develop power in the defense of western Europe against Stalinism. In the first case it allowed what was right in its cause to hide the recklessness of the policy of demanding unconditional surrender, and in the second case it may have exaggerated the danger of a direct military attack on western Europe. The United States is right today in trying to keep as much of the world as possible open so that nations may choose their own social systems. However it does exaggerate the role of military force in this effort and it is guided by a persistent notion of American omnipotence. It clothes its policies with far too simple ideas of freedom and with a too absolutistic anti-Communism.[6]

I come now to a question that is asked on all sides whenever

[6] Why does Bennett omit specific examples of American attitudes and beliefs and depersonalize his objections to United States' policies?

churches and synagogues or their leaders speak about these problems of foreign policy and international relations. Always we hear it said that these high matters belong to the experts or to policy makers on the spot who live with the changing details of the problems and who may have access to classified information. We are often believed to be outsiders who are said to have competence to speak.

It is very difficult to disentangle the moral factors from the technical and, in the broadest sense, strategic factors in any complicated situation. I shall speak of six areas in which persons, who combine religious perspectives and moral sensitivity with a careful attempt to understand the relevant facts even though they are not specialists or insiders in the government, have a duty and right to speak.[7]

First, they have a duty and a right to call attention to the immediate human consequences of any policy. This in itself may not be decisive because there is always the question of the probable human consequences of changing the policy. Yet, this question should not silence the critic. The human consequences of an alternative policy in many cases may be quite speculative and, however one may judge concerning it, what our nation may now be doing to people needs to be kept to the fore.

Second, the determination of the goals of policy is a matter of moral choice. Dean Acheson, in his provocative speech at Amherst College in 1964 about morality and foreign policy, was right in dismissing many moral slogans as inadequate guides to policy, but when he came to his own statement of the goal of American policy he said that our goal was "to preserve and foster an environment in which free societies may exist and flourish." Is not his own phrase "free societies" another one-sided moral slogan? How is this freedom to be related to a transforming justice and to order and to viability in a nation in a period of tumultuous and revolutionary change?

Without taking time for analysis, I shall dogmatically state four goals that should guide our policy. They are all of them moral goals but they are all of them consistent with a wise

[7] Note the order in which Bennett discusses his six major points. How could he have rearranged them to improve the speech?

estimate of the conditions for our own national welfare and security in the long run. They are as follows: (1) the prevention of war and especially the prevention of the escalation of any conflict into general nuclear war; (2) the preservation of as wide an area as possible of openness in the world in which nations have freedom to choose their own social systems, in which there is diversity and mutual respect among those who choose diverse paths; (3) the helping of nations that are struggling against hunger and poverty to achieve justice and access to plenty and to do so in their way and not necessarily in our way; (4) support for the United Nations and development of its functions to enable nations to find their security in multilateral substitutes for the present arms race, to extend the rule of law among nations and to encourage the growth of mutual confidence and humane relations between them. At any given moment there may be a fierce debate among moralists concerning the priority that is to be assigned to each of these goals. This is where morality necessarily becomes contextual. But let no context in which we may be called to act obscure any one of them. The assignment of priorities is not a matter for the expert alone. It does not depend on classified information. It should not be the monopoly of the policy maker. It should be a subject of continuous national discussion to which churches and synagogues can make an essential contribution.

The third area of moral concern has to do with the means used to achieve any or all of these ends. Here there will be much debate among us between those who represent a religious pacifism and those who believe that they must allow for the use of military force to check force or to overcome oppression. I belong to the latter group but the issues are so difficult that I often wish that I did not. For one thing, I am much impressed today by the probability that even uses of force that have some justification easily escalate and, even when this process remains limited, do more harm than good. Can we not agree on two forms of limitation of force? One is that we should not use bombs, nuclear or conventional, against centers of population as was done in the Second World War and as is now being threatened by our own government as a last resort. I know that we are at a stage in which there is plausibility in allowing some license to what may be called "deterrent talk" even though it is murderous. I am not clear about this myself except that I believe that this cannot go on for long without being very much a source of moral corruption to a nation that engages in it. I hope that this subject can be well discussed. The other form of limitation of force is to be resolved never to use nuclear weapons first. There are difficult technical problems here mixed with moral problems, for example, problems involving the differences between types of nuclear weapons and their relation to conventional weapons. Also there has been a very significant movement in American policy away from first use of nuclear weapons that needs to be interpreted and understood.

While we discuss these matters in general terms, we should give strong support to those in our government who resolutely refuse to bomb Hanoi or to extend our bombing to China. If it is true that the President feels stronger pressure from those who would expand the war than he does from those who would restrict it or end it now, whatever else we may think about our policy in Vietnam, we should be able to agree on our responsibility to counteract that pressure.[8]

A fourth area in which religious groups can make a contribution is in helping the American people to see the world as it appears to other countries and especially as it appears to people in Asia and Africa and Latin America, for they get less of a hearing among us than the European nations. Our churches have close relations with the churches in these other continents. What we hear from our fellow churchmen there reflects much more than an inside church point of view; it reflects widely held views in their nations.

Let me give one illustration of this kind of contribution that churches can make to the national discussion about Vietnam. The General Board of the National Council of Churches in a message to the American churches last December put great emphasis on the self-defeating character of our action in

[8] The effectiveness of a speech is often determined by the speaker's ability to make his ideas relevant to contemporary conditions. Do these comments help make the speech more valuable for the audience?

Vietnam because of its effects on the sensibilities of Asians. Here is one very forthright statement:

> We believe that if the United States follows a unilateral policy in Vietnam, no conceivable victory there can compensate for the distrust and hatred of the United States that is being generated each day throughout the world because we are seen as a predominately white nation using our overwhelming military strength to kill more and more Asians.

The Central Committee of the World Council of Churches made a similar statement last month:

> The primary objective must be to stop the fighting as the most effective step to starting discussions and negotiations. This is not an easy task and we are not unaware of the deep rooted obstacles which have thus far prevented progress from the battlefield to the conference table. This is all the more urgent because by continuing the conflict both sides face acute problems. On the one hand the United States of America and its allies face the increase of bitter racial and other resentments against the United States and the West, and on the other hand the Vietnamese face the vast destruction of their people and resources. The prospect of victory at the end of the conflict does not justify this inevitable cost.

I do not suggest that churches have a monopoly of wisdom concerning the more intangible effects of our policies on other peoples, but they do have an inside track to this kind of understanding and it is easy for the policy makers and experts in any one country to be so absorbed with a problem from the point of view that has become dominant in that country to fail to see how self-defeating their policies may be.[9] Also they often gain a vested interest in policies and so, rather than admit an error, they extend the range of their commitment in the hope of proving that they were right. This need not be a conscious process.

The fifth area in which those who are not specialists and those who are not policy makers on the spot may make a contribution has to do with the presuppositions of policy, expressed or unexpressed. Is it not probably true that on impor-

[9] What evidence does Bennett cite to support his claim that churches have special knowledge to offer concerning the people of Africa, Asia, and Latin America? Is this a strong point?

tant matters of foreign policy that go beyond limited tactical decisions, our makers and defenders of policy are governed less by facts, of which they may have a monopoly, than they are by pictures of the world—assumptions about this period of history which they bring to the facts? These pictures of the world and these assumptions are usually shot through with moral judgments, often conventional and unexamined moral judgments. I have in mind assumptions about the dynamics of Communism in its various stages, about the role of military power in the containment of Communism in a revolutionary situation, about the meaning of social revolution on other continents, about the place of freedom in relation to other values, about the limits of American power, about the effect of what we do on the attitudes of other peoples toward us and toward our values, about the relevance of our experience in dealing with Hitler and Stalin in Europe to the way in which we deal with problems in Asia, about the degree of the risk of nuclear war involved in our policy and about our moral right to take such risks. Assumptions on such matters as these are determinative. Military expertise is no guarantee of wisdom about any one of them. And on some of them decisions may be made on the highest level on the basis of an unexamined line of thought that has become dominant. Churches and synagogues have no monopoly of wisdom about these matters either, but they do have their contribution to make to the discernment of misuses of religion and morality in relation to them. These issues belong to the sphere of public debate. They need the widest possible ventilation from all sides with many voices heard from other countries. I believe that at the present time in the context of our policy, especially in relation to Asia and Latin America, our policy makers are in a rut in their public positions about many of these issues. For this reason I hope that they can receive a great deal of frank discussion at this Conference.

A final contribution that churches and synagogues can make to the national discussion of these issues is to criticize the false uses of religion and morality that are so pervasive. This means criticism of the psychology of the holy war that is one factor in the American attitude toward the cold war. This means alertness about all forms of national self-righteousness. It also calls for a continuous examination of the use of such words as "honor," "obligation" and "commitment" when our policy in Vietnam is defended by spokesmen of government. Honor is an especially ambiguous word and it is difficult to distinguish between its use to refer to national "face-saving" and its use to refer to a genuine moral obligation.

I shall limit myself to a discussion of one issue that seems to be most pervasive, and that is the view that we hold of Communism. At the present time in many situations one major source of error in the determination of policy is an absolutistic anti-Communism. I do not believe that this is always so, for in relation to European Communism this outlook has been in large measure abandoned. The breaking of the Communist monolith by the Sino-Soviet split, the gradual humanization of society in the Soviet Union and most of the eastern European Communist countries, the diverse paths taken by these eastern European nations—these developments fortunately have influenced American policy. We now know intellectually, even if this knowledge is not fully absorbed, that for a nation to become Communist does not mean that it is lost for all time to Stalinist slavery. The American rhetoric of a decade ago that kept contrasting the free world with the slave world has fortunately disappeared in the highest circles of government though its influence remains to a considerable extent on the public.

No influence has been more helpful in counteracting the American anti-Communist obsession than Pope John XXIII and the Vatican Council. Pope John did much to expel the holy war psychology in relation to Communism from his Church and from other churches. It is most significant that the Vatican Council refused to take action condemning Communism and that it initiated steps leading to dialogue with atheists, Marxist atheists and others.

Yet the American obsession with anti-Communism keeps appearing, especially when we seem on the point at times of declaring that we have responsibility to oppose all wars of liberation in Asia and Latin America if they are inspired by one of the branches of international Communism.

I believe that we should help nations that can be helped to find alternatives to Communism because, however much a Communist society may improve after some decades, it does bring terror and tyranny in the early stages to any country that embraces it. I do think that we should put over against this fact the recognition that Communists have no monopoly of terror. The recent slaughter of Communists in Indonesia by the scores if not hundreds of thousands should remind us of this. Political cruelty on all sides in tumultuous situations is so common that it should perhaps gain our attention more than it does. We have a habit of remembering the atrocities of our adversaries and forgetting those of our friends. But this is an aside. The axiom that Communism is the worst fate that can ever come to any country is false. It may not be worse than years and years of civil war; it may not be worse than some rightist tyrannies; it may not be worse than decades or even generations of neglected social and economic problems. Communism is cruel in its early stages and it has not been successful in dealing with all problems, the problem of agriculture for example, but after the revolutionary period it does become in many ways constructive: it does overcome anarchy, it does deal radically with famine and poverty and disease and illiteracy. If it can be gradually humanized, as has proved to be the case in European Communist countries, our nation should not assume the responsibility to take all measures to prevent a nation in Asia from becoming Communist. The answer may be that they will be allowed to vote themselves into Communism but how far self-determination in this sense can be a reality in situations of civil war and revolution is debatable. One fine day there might be a free election but what is to prevent its results from being overturned six months later? The pressure and counterpressure of political movements in such situations seem to determine the fate of nations whether there are elections or not. We in America do not like to have it so, but there are some things that are beyond our control and when we try to control them we may do far more harm than good, even if our motives are the best.[10]

[10] This is probably the most controversial paragraph in Bennett's speech. Does he offer adequate support for his belief that communism is not the worst fate that can come to a country?

I cannot speak of Communism without dealing with China. As we face the reality of China as a vast human power, whether it is moved primarily by Communism or by nationalism, churches and synagogues have no expert knowledge of what is happening in that country; nor can they read the minds of the Chinese leaders, those who will soon pass from the scene or those soon to assume power. The doctrines and slogans of the Chinese which seem to scare our Defense Department are paranoiac even though, so far, Chinese behavior has been prudent and cautious. Who is to decide how significant the doctrines and the slogans are? Mr. James Reston raises the question as to whether this is for the Defense Department to decide. Certainly this conference is in no position to decide. However, I think that we can emphasize the following considerations.

Communism has been the instrument by which China has been unified, by which it has become able to assert itself among the nations, by which it has been able to purge itself of the effects of generations of humiliation at the hands of the white West. Why must we take all that China does now against us with such seriousness, and forget for how long she has been the victim of the Western powers of which this nation is now the chief representative? Why must we have such a double standard that we allow ourselves to do, near the borders of China, what we would never allow China to do near our borders? Why are we still involved in the Chinese civil war as the major ally of Nationalist China? Is there no possibility of our changing our attitudes toward China, even though we know that a tragic history and the fanaticism of early Communism make it unlikely that China will soon change her attitude toward us? How long are we to be engaged in diplomatic efforts to keep Communist China isolated? Should our policy not be designed with all the imagination we can muster to undercut the paranoia of China and not to exacerbate it as is now the case with everything that we do or leave undone?

In our religious communities there should be continual efforts to counteract national attitudes in regard to China. The General Board of the National Council of Churches called recently for a reversal of American policies that are designed to isolate China and for preparation for the widest variety of relations between the United States and China.

China today is relatively weak. If we take advantage of her weakness to keep her down and deny her even her natural role as the greatest power in Asia, a role that we assume for ourselves in this hemisphere, if we isolate her and continue to express our own hostility against her, punctuated by moral lectures about what is the result of a tragic history to which the great powers of the West have contributed so much, we may find ourselves face to face fifteen years from now with a powerful China that has every reason to seek revenge upon us. I do not say that this prospect should be the main motive for a change of attitude and a change of policy, but it does indicate the kind of judgment that will come upon us if we do not do so. Churches and synagogues should provide an environment in our country within which these questions are continually raised and in which new attitudes can begin to form. I hope and pray that new relationships will become possible between our religious communities and the people of mainland China. We often hear that our government would like to change its policy in many respects but that it is afraid of the people. If so, let us do what we can among the people to support its desire for change and let us ask the representatives of government to give some leadership if they do seek freedom to change.

One final word. I have said very little in this address about the United Nations and the institutions of world order, but I believe that churches and synagogues should not only give strong support to the United Nations and to the efforts to improve its working but should, as of now, put great stress on the need for multilateral judgments upon American actions. The United States get some support for its Asian policies from its European allies and from nations on the eastern fringe of Asia and, doubtless, it is always easy to find people around the world who are somewhat ambivalent because they see in the power of the United States the only countervailing power east of Suez. But let us not expect very much of this support and let us not allow it to lead to self-justification. Whatever any one here may think of American policy to date in Vietnam, there is a terribly dangerous momentum in our power. We may easily become its prisoner. Also the mounting of national self-justification may gradually cause the self-criticism that now exists to erode. There is danger that more complete moral isolation is not far away. Unless we find ways to submit our policies that affect all mankind to a far broader judgment than is now the case we may become a nation possessed by a destructive determination to have our own way in Asia. Our religious communities are called to be an inner check on this development. This first Interfaith Conference dealing with these issues should begin to prepare us to meet this call.

CRITICAL ANALYSIS AND PROJECTS

1. What strategy does Bennett employ to unify his audience before discussing the six major points of his speech?
2. Since delegates to the conference undoubtedly already shared Bennett's belief in the right and duty of the church to speak out, what possible explanations can you offer for his emphasis of this point?
3. In what ways do Bennett's views toward communism differ from Dougherty's?
4. What purpose does Bennett's detailed discussion of Communist China serve in this speech?
5. What are the functions of the rhetorical questions in this speech? What other stylistic devices are used?
6. Prepare a speech in which you describe the dilemmas that communism poses for the Christian.
7. Assist your teacher in organizing a symposium on the growing influence of Communist China upon world peace. Select the speakers from among the professors on your campus who have special knowledge about this question.

SELECTED BIBLIOGRAPHY

1. Bainton, Roland H. *Christian Attitudes Towards War and Peace.* Nashville, Tenn.: Abingdon Press, 1960.
2. Bennett, John C. *Moral Tensions in International Affairs.* New York: Council in Religion and International Affairs, 1964.
3. ———. *Nuclear Weapons and the Conflict of Conscience.* New York: Scribner, 1962.
4. ———, *et al. The Road to Peace.* Philadelphia: Fortress Press, 1966.
5. Brown, Robert M., *et al. Vietnam: Crisis of Conscience.* New York: Association Press, 1967.
6. Finn, James. *Protest: Pacifism and Politics.* New York: Random House, 1968.
7. ———, ed. *Peace, the Churches, and the Bomb.* New York: Council in Religion and International Affairs, 1965.
8. Glazer, Nathan. "The Peace Movement in America—1961," *Commentary,* XXXI (April 1961) , 288–296.
9. Hamilton, Michael P., ed. *The Vietnam War: Christian Perspectives.* Grand Rapids, Mich.: William B. Eerdsmans Publishing Co., 1967.
10. Jennings, James R. "Churches in Foreign Policy Debates," *Worldview,* XI (March 1968) , 6–7.
11. "Western Values and Total War," *Commentary,* XXXII (October 1961) , 277–304.

PART FOUR

SOLDIERS AND PEACE

VII

JAMES M. GAVIN

Vietnam and Global Commitments

The decade of the 1960s reminded Americans that peace has a peculiar way of disappearing. Research and speeches directed at strengthening and preserving peace-keeping procedures suddenly had to be redirected toward stopping the shooting in Vietnam. Numerous Americans protested their country's military action, but few were prepared to offer a military strategy, short of complete withdrawal, which would alter the escalation of the war. Vietnam critics found the help they needed in a letter written by Lieutenant General James M. Gavin (retired) to *Harper's Magazine*, February 1966.[1] Stressing that he was writing "from a military-technical point of view," General Gavin urged that American troops be withdrawn from scattered areas in South Vietnam and assigned to defend a limited number of enclaves along the South Vietnam coast.[2]

Because he had opposed Eisenhower's plan of scaling down conventional forces, Gavin retired from a distinguished military career in 1958 and became vice-president of Arthur D. Little, Inc. He served as United States ambassador to France

Reprinted from *Hearings Before the Committee on Foreign Relations,* United States Senate, 89th Cong., 2nd Sess., Pt. 1. (February 26, 1966), 226–235.

[1] "A Communication on Vietnam," *Harper's Magazine,* CCXXXII (February 1966), 12, 18, 21.

[2] *Ibid.,* p. 16.

under the Kennedy administration, but had returned to Arthur D. Little as chairman of the board by the time he appeared before the Senate committee investigating United States' policy in Vietnam.

On February 8, 1966, General Gavin went before Senator J. William Fulbright's Committee on Foreign Relations and for five hours stated his views on Vietnam with the same candor that characterized his disagreement with the Eisenhower administration in 1958. General Gavin's testimony was carried live by the NBC and CBS television networks. The following remarks are his opening statement and the beginning of a question and answer period. Pennsylvania's Senator Joseph Clark recognized the impact of General Gavin's testimony when he commented, "The policy of non-escalation has now become respectable."[3]

May I say, sir, at the outset, that in the background of my point of view that I have arrived at and expressed in that communication to *Harper's* magazine went 2 years of service with the Philippine Scouts in the late thirties, and since that time considerable interest in the affairs of southeast Asia.

At the time of the fall of Dienbienphu, at the direction of the Chief of Staff, I visited Korea, Formosa, Saigon, talked to Diem, talked to General Ely there, General Collins, General Daniels, and others about the problems; went on to Thailand and talked to Mr. Sarit.

Among other things at that time I recommended the construction of a highway from Bangkok to the Mekong, feeling that Thailand was a very sensitive spot and very likely might become a very deeply involved part of the southeast Asia—deeply involved in our own strategy and affairs.

Since then, perhaps one of the most interesting experiences I have had was with Mr. Kennedy. About a month after going to the post in Paris he asked me to return to talk about the

[3] "The Senate Hearings," *Newsweek*, LXVII (February 21, 1966), 27.

problems of Laos. He was confronted with a very difficult situation, and I speak from memory now. We were supporting Phoumi, a rightist, and the question confronting President Kennedy was to what extent should we become involved in land warfare in Laos.

I do not know, but I would suspect if he had sought the advice of the Pentagon, we no doubt would have committed forces and ultimately more divisions and more divisions. But to Mr. Kennedy this made little sense and, indeed, the more we talked about it, the more I agreed with him, a landlocked country, remote from the immediate application of seapower and somewhat less of airpower seemed to offer a hopeless situation to us.

He asked me, therefore, to go to Paris upon my return and enter into discussions with Souvanna Phouma to see if we could not convince that gentleman that we were interested in a "free, neutral, independent Laos." This I undertook to do.

Admittedly it was with some misgivings at the outset because Souvanna Phouma had a reputation of being then very close to the Communists, and I was not at all sure of how our negotiations would come out.

Mr. Harriman very ably conducted negotiations in Geneva in parallel with my own discussions in Paris.

After about six or eight meetings, and very fruitful and fascinating meetings they were for me, we did arrive indeed at a treaty that, hopefully guaranteed the freedom, neutrality, and independence of Laos.[4]

I was aware then, as I am now, that what our President sought to achieve was a political settlement to what appeared to be a potentially serious military problem. He was absolutely right. He was absolutely right, and we did arrive at that solution.

Since then I have continued to devote a great deal of my time to matters of global strategy in our commitments.

Last summer I was asked, late last spring I was asked, by the

[4] What is the net effect of Gavin's testimony up to this point? Has he established his position as an authority on Southeast Asia?

New York Times to do an article on the meaning of the atomic bomb 20 years later. This was for the early August edition of the New York Times magazine. I had given a great deal of attention to the bombing in 1940, and even then came to the conclusion that urban bombing lacked credibility for a number of reasons perhaps not worthwhile going into here, and I wrote an article that I was denied publication at that time. I felt that the problems of the bomb were quite different than simply escalating World War II experience into more and more and more applied power.

As the summer of 1965 came to an end, my thinking on this matter formed into real meaning of the changes in global strategy that in my opinion have taken place in the last 20 years, and I did an article on this, and in the midst of this I was exchanging correspondence with Mr. Fisher, talking about air cavalry which was a postulation advanced in the early 1950's, considered far too radical for acceptance at the time, and now has valid and accepted battlefield application.

So I at that time and late in the summer or early fall decided that in view of our total spectrum of global commitments, and the changing nature of global strategy, we had better look hard at our Vietnamese commitment. It was becoming alarmingly out of balance and this was the basis for the letter I wrote which I will be very happy to come back to later.

I might say that all I said in that letter was let's look at (*a*) where we are today, what our commitments are, what it is costing and what we do; and (*b*) what the alternatives are, what these costs might be, and having done this, let's make up our mind what we are going to do.

My feeling was that we were being escalated at the will of opponents rather than at our own judgment, and I based this as much upon the statement of many officials who have been to that war-torn country and who returned with optimistic statements only to find they have had to change them successively thereafter, which suggested to me that in the very beginning they didn't understand what the requirements were and thus couldn't estimate accurately what the needs might be to meet those requirements.

In that letter I, too, in passing made reference to Hanoi and Peiping and the futility of bombing, pointing out that just more of this would cause more problems, create more problems than it would solve.

I referred specifically to "urban bombing." I would like to make that clear.[5]

THE CHAIRMAN. Is this still in 1962, General?

GENERAL GAVIN. I beg your pardon.

THE CHAIRMAN. I just wanted to place this in time. Was this in 1962?

GENERAL GAVIN. No; this was late last year.

THE CHAIRMAN. Last year; I am sorry.

GENERAL GAVIN. Late last year, and Harper's came out about my thinking of the strategy which I would like to talk about briefly. At the moment I am, in passing, touching upon the letter.

I have a feeling as our bombing went on beyond what were obviously military targets such as ammunition dumps, tank cars or concentrations of trucks and military targets, to powerplants and such as that, we were slowly creeping to urban bombing. I wanted to lay this at rest for once and for all time.

Just bombing a city per se, for psychological reasons achieves little in the way of military effect and, in fact, today in the court of world opinion could be extremely damaging and we would have nothing to show for it, and I want to be sure to head that off, that in my own opinion just bombing Peiping wouldn't serve anything.

Now, sir, if I may talk a little about the matter of global strategy into which I would like to fit Vietnam. Two of the most significant things that have happened in our time certainly have been the bomb and the space exploration. Both of which have tremendous military significance.

[5] Gavin's testimony thus far has been a narration of his previous views and activities. Would his presentation have been more effective if he had stated basic arguments and supported them with evidence instead of personal opinion?

The bomb is a very interesting case in point. The first question we asked ourselves was the meaning of the bomb. Was the bomb the beginning of a new age, in which the atom would solve our military problems that we have been unable to solve in the past by other means, or was it indeed the end?

I suspected at first that it was the end, although this was a very minority opinion and now I am absolutely satisfied that it was. As man has sought to impose his will on an opponent from the beginning of recorded history he has sought to use energy in every form that he could get it, bludgeon, metallic penetrating instruments, metallic pellets fired by chemical charges to the explosion of the fission of the atom and fusion of the atom itself. He finally has succeeded in bringing down to the earth the very explosions that take place on the surface of the sun, fission. He has brought the energy of the cosmos itself to the earth. He no longer can use it because it could destroy a major segment of the human race. He is at the end of the search for energy with which to impose his will on fellow men. He is at the end; that search has terminated. Now he must find more discreet means, more discriminating means. He must find greater mobility, rapid data transmission, he must keep these weapons under control. He must know what is going on everywhere as quickly as he can find out so as to keep under control local conflagrations and thus avoid the major catastrophe that might occur if, thoughtlessly, nuclear weapons were used.[6]

If this is so, and it is purely a concept in which I do not ask you to share agreement but I am grateful for the opportunity of expressing it; if this is so, then for the first time in human history something very unusual is happening in warfare and I believe indeed it is.

Strategy has to do with those measures which taken short of war that makes absolute victory certain. If war occurs inadvertently you are sure to win.

It seems to me the best analysis I have been able to make . . .

[6] Does this material need to be included, or does it interfere with more relevant testimony?

SENATOR SYMINGTON. Excuse me, what was that, if war occurs inadvertently; I didn't understand.

GENERAL GAVIN. If a war occurs inadvertently, if your strategy is right you are going to win and I will give you an example of that, Mr. Symington.

I might say, if I may, that I have given a great deal of thought and done some writing on the subject. I taught political science at the University of California, 4 weeks in 1946 on a sabbatical, and I haven't come to these conclusions rather casually. They represent for me, at least, considerable effort and thought.

It seems to me, therefore, that our strategy today should be based upon, first of all, a dynamic and viable prospering economy, an economy that can export entrepreneurial skills, managerial techniques, dollars for acquisition, ventures abroad, to help other people. We have developed a way of life that provides an abundance of means for our people, and we should continue to export this just as aggressively as we can to help other people.

I am not talking about economic colonialism, for the enlightened businessman working abroad today is trying to help other people help themselves. People are not born equal nor indeed are nations born equal and they need help to achieve a place for their people. They need help of many kinds. We have been doing extremely well in this respect.

While I am talking in this context of strategy, it seems to me, for example, if one of these great books on decisive battles, "Fifteen Decisive Battles of the World," by Sir Edward S. Creasy, were to be rewritten today it would include the demise of Mr. Khrushchev, who sought to coexist with his own totalitarian system organized on the basis of planning and not on market demand, who failed because he simply couldn't get the grain grown, he didn't have fertilizer and his economy just simply couldn't produce, and characteristically as happens in a failing strategy he sought the tactical gambit to recoup. He went to Cuba in a great adventure that, thanks to our great President, and our Secretary of Defense, he was defeated in.

I would say that his demise is one of the decisive setbacks in all history, and I think now in my personal opinion, that our efforts to work closely with the Soviet people should be rewarding, in fact I believe that in the President's state of the Union message the references to making changes in our tariff laws to encourage trade is a very good thing.

We have done a great deal exporting professors, entertainers, and scientists, now export businessmen and their techniques. I think we can go a long way together.

There was a turning point and it was the demise of Mr. Khrushchev.

Well now, I would say further that strategy today is in the realm of science and technology. Out of science and an adequate research program we are producing an abundance of new knowledge that will energize our economy and keep it moving and, very briefly, I think that in the court of world opinion, world opinion itself, we have the area that will have a very great deal to do with what we may do.

I would draw a parallel of the use of energy and power through the many, many centuries of human existence when people were restrained by their fellow men in what they could do. They may have wanted to do many things. Even cities, States restrained what their armed forces could do, and this Nation has shrunk, this world has shrunk to the point today, this world has shrunk to the point today where we simply can't do all the things we would like to do.

I have always felt that one of our greatest captains of all time was General MacArthur and yet even he had to come to realize and learn the hard way that the use of a nuclear bomb, because we had them in our arsenal, did not permit him under his mandate from the United Nations to use it.

It was simply an intolerable thing.

I have touched on three areas of strategy that I believe are of overriding importance.

My concern, therefore, for Vietnam first became aroused when I found us cutting back in our global commitments in the realm of economics, for I began to suspect that the escalation in southeast Asia would begin to hurt our world strategic position. If this has significance now it may have tremendous significance in the long run. When we begin to turn back on what we are doing in world affairs, through our economic endeavors, to support a tactical confrontation that appears to be escalating at the will of an enemy we are in a very dangerous position in my opinion, and for this reason what we are doing there deserves looking at.

There are several areas where confrontations occur tactically. I mentioned Cuba. Europe is one today, in my opinion. Our commitments in Europe are far in excess of our needs, not only troop commitments but logistical support to back up those commitments.

To return to Asia, the Korean commitment is one we must maintain, and we are maintaining it. The support of Chiang Kai-shek, Taiwan, the offshore islands of Quemoy and Matsu likewise. Southeast Asia is a very volatile, dynamic area of operations. Vietnam is not alone. Thailand I look upon as a very, very dangerous area and one that we should regard most seriously at this time.

Therefore, in looking at it, I raise some questions.

First of all, what do we have today and what can they do, and I simply stated today we have sufficient forces in South Vietnam to hold areas along the coast where sea and air power can be made fully effective, and then we can use this power as we see fit to do so, I then suggested that we might look at the alternatives very realistically.

Are we really trying to seal off Vietnam entirely, extend the 17th parallel all across, all the way across to the Mekong River? This has been considered. One could put a cordon sanitaire across there at considerable cost. It would still be open ended a bit at the end but it is possible.

One could extend the security down to the Cambodian border but to me these appear to be terribly costly in manpower and our national wealth, and I use the word "wealth" to include all necessary material resources.

So I finally came to the conclusion, and I think this is very important in view of the charges that have been made about what I have said, and I quote "We must do the best we can with the forces we have deployed in Vietnam now." Nothing more than that. I did not say "withdraw," "retreat," "go ahead," "attack," do anything else.[7] We must do the best we can with what we have in hand, keeping in mind the true meaning of global strategy in world affairs today.

Economics, science and technology, and world opinion will, in the long run, serve our strategic interests well if we handle our national resources wisely.

On the other hand; tactical mistakes that are allowed to escalate at the initiative of an enemy could be disastrously costly. Since the advent of the space age there has been a revolution in the nature of global conflict. The confrontation in Vietnam is the first test of our understanding of such change or lack of it. The measures that we now take in southeast Asia must stem from sagacity and thoughtfulness, restraint and an awareness of the nature of strategy in this very rapidly shrinking world, and that is right from the letter that I wrote to Harper's.

Now, Mr. Chairman, perhaps at this point, I might say nothing further and I would be very pleased to have an opportunity to answer any questions that may be addressed to me.

THE CHAIRMAN. Thank you very much, General.

I think your review of the overall strategy is very useful. Speaking for myself, not being a military man, it has great appeal but I won't wish to pass judgment on it further than that.

I believe, General, you had something to do with the study of Indochina in 1954 when you were working with General Ridgway.

GENERAL GAVIN. Yes, sir, I was the Chief of Plans and Development beginning in early 1954 and I stayed in that position and then in research for several years.

THE CHAIRMAN. Did you participate in the study that General Ridgway ordered relative to the feasibility of at that time of entering the conflict in Indochina?

7 Why does Gavin take special care also to state what strategy he is not advocating in Vietnam?

GENERAL GAVIN. Yes, Mr. Chairman. We considered the advisability of entering the Hanoi Delta, and as I recall, to be precise, we talked about the need for some 8 divisions, plus some 35 engineer battalions, we anticipated the supply would be very great, medical and so on, and there was some significance to Hainan Island if we were going to go into the delta and so on, we gave it quite thorough consideration.

THE CHAIRMAN. In General Ridgway's book, "The Soldier," on page 276 he said this, and I would read it and see if you would comment on General Ridgway's statement:

> I felt it was essential, therefore, that all who had any influence in making the decision on this grave matter should be fully aware of all the factors involved. To provide these facts, I sent out to Indochina an Army team of experts in every field; engineers, signal and communication specialists, medical officers, and experienced combat leaders who knew how to evaluate terrain in terms of battle tactics. * * * The area, they found, was practically devoid of those facilities which modern forces such as ours find essential to the waging of war. Its telecommunications, highways, railways—all the things that make possible the operation of a modern combat force on land—were almost nonexistent. Its port facilities and airfields were totally inadequate and to provide the facilities we would need would require tremendous engineering and logistical efforts.

On page 277 he writes:

> We could have fought Indochina. We could have won, if we had been willing to pay the tremendous cost in men and money that such intervention would have required—a cost that in my opinion would have eventually been as great as, or greater than, that we paid in Korea. In Korea, we had learned that air and naval power alone cannot win a war and that inadequate ground forces cannot win one either. It was incredible to me that we had forgotten the bitter lesson so soon—that we were on the verge of making that same tragic error.
>
> That error, thank God, was not repeated. As soon as the full report was in, I lost no time in having it passed on up the chain of command. It reached President Eisenhower. To a man of his military experience its implications were immediately clear. The idea of intervention was abandoned, and it is my belief that the analysis which the Army made and presented to higher authority played a considerable, perhaps a decisive, part in persuading our Government not to embark on that tragic adventure.

General, are the conditions in Indochina any different today than they were at that time?

GENERAL GAVIN. There is one basic difference, sir. He was talking about going into the Hanoi Delta and going right to the Chinese frontier, which certainly meant the immediate intervention of Chinese opposition. Now we are considerably farther south, we are talking about the 17th parallel on down. Other than that I would say conditions are not essentially different, although the point I make is a very important one, too.

I should say, too, in the way of background there is more than just a cold piece of paper in this type of planning. We spent a lot of time worrying about it, certainly I did.

I had considerable combat experience in Europe from Africa to Berlin, and I knew that I would be responsible for planning the conduct of operations, and I devoted a great deal of talk about it with colleagues who had considerable experience in southeast Asia and China.

We finally decided when we were all through what we were talking about doing was going to war with Red China under conditions that were appallingly disadvantageous. We were talking about going to war with her thousands and thousands of miles from the heart of our warmaking capacity and it frankly made little sense to a man who had to go do the fighting. So I was more than pleased to see General Ridgway take the initiative and it took more courage to do it as he did and say "Let's take a look at this. It makes little sense to do it."

THE CHAIRMAN. Do you think the conditions in South Vietnam—the conditions mentioned in this book—are any more favorable to the conduct of war than in North Vietnam? Is the terrain more favorable? Are the conditions of health more favorable?[8]

GENERAL GAVIN. No.

[8] How does Senator Fulbright take advantage of Gavin's appearance to establish some basic points? Is this kind of exchange more effective than a persuasive speech?

CRITICAL ANALYSIS AND PROJECTS

1. General Gavin drew much criticism immediately after he published his letter in *Harper's Magazine*. What method of refutation does he rely upon in his opening remarks? Are his appeals intended to affect the committee or the national television audience?
2. What effect do the interruptions of Senator Fulbright and Senator Symington have upon the clarity of the speech?
3. General Gavin seemed to be speaking without a prepared text. What evidence can you find in the transcript of the speech to support that observation?
4. How does General Gavin's discussion of global strategy relate to his views on what should be done in Vietnam?
5. What technique did Senator Fulbright use in the questioning period to enable General Gavin to attack current military strategy? Is it an ethical procedure?
6. An American critic of his government's foreign policy risks the charge of being called unpatriotic, especially if he calls for a change in military policy during a war. Organize a panel discussion for your class in which the freedoms and responsibilities of dissenters are analyzed.
7. Read item 1. in the bibliography and prepare a speech showing what role public speaking might play in a political protest movement conforming to Boulding's standards.

SELECTED BIBLIOGRAPHY

1. Boulding, Kenneth E. "Reflections on Protest," *Bulletin of Atomic Scientists,* XXI (October 1965), 18–20.
2. Fall, Bernard B. *The Two Viet-Nams: A Political and Military Analysis.* 2nd rev. ed. New York: Frederick A. Praeger, 1967.
3. Gavin, James M. *War and Peace in the Space Age.* New York: Harper and Row, 1958.
4. ———. "The Weapons of 1984," *Saturday Review,* LI (August 31, 1968), 13–15, 39–40.
5. ———, and Arthur T. Hadley. *Crisis Now.* New York: Random House, 1968.

6. Gruening, Senator Ernest, and Herbert W. Beaser. *Vietnam Folly*. Washington, D.C.: The National Press, Inc., 1968.
7. Halperin, Morton H. *Limited War in the Nuclear Age*. New York: John Wiley and Sons, 1963.
8. Kennedy, John F. "General Gavin Sounds the Alarm," *Reporter*, XIX (October 30, 1958) , 35–36.
9. McClintock, Robert. *The Meaning of Limited War*. Boston: Houghton Mifflin Co., 1967.
10. Society of Friends, American Friends Service Committee. *Peace in Vietnam*. New York: Hill and Wang, 1966.

VIII

EARLE G. WHEELER

The Challenge Came in Vietnam

Under most administrations, generals have not been permitted to criticize foreign policy, and rarely have they chosen to debate the opponents of American policy. The conflict in Vietnam, however, has changed all that. The general is now as important at the rostrum as he is on the battlefield. A frequent defender of United States' policy in Vietnam is General Earle G. Wheeler, chairman of the Joint Chiefs of Staff, the highest military post in the United States.[1]

General Wheeler was appointed army chief of staff under the Kennedy administration. A close friend of the President and of Secretary of Defense McNamara, General Wheeler gave his support to the nuclear test-ban treaty in 1963. Under the Johnson administration he maintained his key role as chief military adviser to the President, the National Security Council, and the Secretary of Defense.

After General Gavin announced his strategy for handling Vietnam in the famous *Harper's Magazine* letter, General Wheeler rejected his views and pointed out that current military policy had been arrived at after high-level consideration of all alternatives. Furthermore, he saw no reason to halt the bombing of North Vietnam since such action represented one of the "three blue chips" for negotiations.[2]

Reprinted by permission from *Vital Speeches of the Day* (December 15, 1966), pp. 130–133.

[1] See, for example, General Wheeler's "Vietnam: A Military Appraisal," *Vital Speeches of the Day,* XXXIV (August 1, 1968), 613–615.

[2] "Gavin Plan Will Not Work," *U.S. News and World Report,* LX (February 7, 1966), 28.

As Americans grew more divided over their country's commitments to Vietnam, General Wheeler chose the Inter-House Council of Brown University as the place to defend administration policy. He spoke on November 15, 1966.

I genuinely appreciate this opportunity to speak to the members of the Inter-House Council of Brown University and their guests. I am pleased that we shall have the chance to exchange views in a question-and-answer period to follow. Although my duties require a great deal of study and discussion of major problems facing our Government, my opportunities for discussion with young Americans are all too infrequent.

Having shed my uniform for this occasion, I trust that I shall fare better than the uncertain soldier in our most un-Civil War who, figuring to play it safe, dressed himself in a blue coat and grey pants, and tiptoed onto the battlefield. He got shot from both directions![3]

By now, much has been said about our involvement in Vietnam. Some comment has been constructive, some destructive; some accurate, and some misleading. Although the volume and variety have been great, I have chosen tonight to add some of my own observations on Vietnam. I do so for three reasons:

First, no group of Americans has such a personal stake, present and future, in Vietnam as those of your generation. Therefore, no group has a more valid right to ask about our involvement.

Second, no issue before this nation is more important, or more far-reaching in both its national and international implications.

And third, no subject has had the pertinent so obscured by the irrelevant, the facts so confused with fancy.[4]

Questions about our role in Southeast Asia often begin

[3] Evaluate Wheeler's decision to appear in civilian clothes as a strategy for overcoming possible hostile reaction to him.

[4] What value is there in a speaker's telling his listeners how he has partitioned the speech?

simply, sincerely, but naively I think, like this: "What are we doing in Vietnam? It's ten thousand miles away!"

First of all, such a question is indicative of the somewhat provincial East Coast–Atlantic Ocean orientation which has traditionally colored our attitudes toward Asia. Vietnam is, indeed, far away. But it is much less than 10,000 miles from those who live on our West Coast, and far closer still to those who live in our 50th state of Hawaii. The fact is the United States is, as it has been for decades, as much a Pacific as an Atlantic nation.

More fundamentally, though, the question of distance or nearness to Vietnam must be measured in newly-scaled terms. We live now in a world rapidly grown small. It is also a world which is much more crowded than it used to be. In today's world, no man can be a total stranger to another; Shangri-La has disappeared into the mists from which it came. The nature and import of this change are worth reflection, for all men are affected by it, and none more than we Americans.

You are familiar, I am sure, with the growth trend in population. In 1650, after millions of years of existence, the earth is estimated to have held only some one-half billion people. By 1850, a short 200 years later, the population had doubled to one billion. By 1960, at least three billion people were trying to live in the same space, and the trend continues.

This population growth alone was bound to change our world—food and elbow room became pressing problems. But the effects of this change have been compounded manifold by discoveries and technological achievements of relatively recent vintage. Think back just a short time in the span of man's existence.

Most of the great names in exploration are connected with the period less than 500 years past—Columbus, Magellan and Cook, to cite a few. Until their time, and even more recently, many of the world's communities were ignorant of each other, wholly separated by geographical barriers. Both between and within nations, there was substantial isolation because people were fewer and means of travel and communication were limited. In 1750, it took eight days to go by coach from Edinburgh to London. It took six days for news of George

Washington's first election to go from Philadelphia to Boston, and six weeks to reach Paris. And it is told that President Jefferson, irked because he had had no word for a year from our ambassador to Spain, threatened to write the ambassador a letter himself if he did not hear within another six months!

It was not until the Civil War that the telegraph first came into widespread use; the first telephone exchange came along in 1878; and radio only 50 years ago.[5]

As a soldier, I must note, too, that weapons were as limited as the means of communication. For most of man's combative history, he has been confronted with weapons of only limited range and destructiveness—the hand-held club and javelin, torches thrown a few hundred feet by cumbersome machines, arrows launched a few hundred yards, and finally explosive shells which could be launched to a distance of a few miles.

Thus, virtually until this century, the earth had ample room for individuals and for whole nations. There was little contact and much ignorance of each other among the separated communities around the globe. To make any contact, either for peace, trade, or war, one had to move physically from one area to another, and movement could only be accomplished with difficulty over a considerable period of time.

I emphasize these circumstances, and the fact that they existed until "only yesterday," to underline by contrast the scope and pace of change in this century. In the past 60 years, while the inhabitants of the earth have doubled, we have all been drawn together by a series of technological developments: radio, photography and television; submarines and aircraft carriers; airplanes and space satellites; and the ominous coupling of missiles with nuclear power. Any one of these might have been enough to end isolation; in sum, they have revolutionized the relationships of man.

Much of this rapid and sometimes chaotic change has come within the span of your life times, since World War II, and it has been as much political, economic and social, as it has been technological.

At the end of World War II, much of the earth lay prostrate

[5] What improvements are needed in this segment?

under the debris of conflict. Governments and nations were in disarray. Colonial empires were fragmented. The social fabric was rent, and millions of human beings were displaced. Industries were halted or destroyed. Jobs were scarce; food was scarcer; and hope perhaps scarcest of all.

The airplane, as I have noted, had come into its own. In war, it was a terrifying instrument; in peace, it foreshortened distances and left no men or places isolated on earth.

There had also been a revolution in communications. The printed, spoken, and pictured word moved 'round the globe, bringing new ideas and new expectations. Significantly, these expectations were rising, above all, in the hearts of men in colonial lands. Now, almost for the first time, these people were beginning to ask for a better share of the world's wealth, and for freedom.

At this moment of awakening, another force, long fermenting, rose to view in major dimension and significance. Communism, given new strength and stature by Russian war victories, renewed its international thrust. Its aim was clearly apparent—to dominate the world scene. Its tactic was twofold: subvert the industrialized nations, and fill the power vacuum in once-colonial lands.

In this broad, postwar context, the United States alone had the residual wealth, strength, and spirit to take the initiative on behalf of the free nations. However reluctantly, it moved to assume this leadership. The world's problems were now the problems of America. As one foreign observer commented, "the United States has world-wide responsibilities without having imperial aspirations."

In assuming this burden, it soon became clear that we had entered into a continuing struggle. On the one side were those countries who wanted to create a decent world order in which nations could freely choose their own institutions, and live in peace with each other. On the other side were those whose aim was a world of one political and economic system for all.[6]

Long before the Vietnam aggression, the free nations had to

[6] How does Wheeler's description of world conditions affect his strategy for justifying American involvement in Vietnam?

confront the aggressive thrust of communism. Those who puzzle about Vietnam today would be less puzzled, I think, if they were first to recall, and study, what happened in Iran, Greece, Berlin, South Korea, the Philippines, Taiwan and Malaya, during the past two decades. Had we and our allies not resisted agression in these lands, how free would their peoples be today, and what kind of a world would we be living in?

In essence, in my judgment, Vietnam is an extension of this struggle which has been imposed upon the free peoples for twenty years. Some find this difficult to comprehend or accept because of the underlying complexities in Vietnam.

Vietnam is a nation whose historical division into the kingdoms of Tonkin, Annam and Cochin China has left long-standing rivalries even to this day. It is a land of ethnic difference, with Vietnamese predominating, but with a substantial mixture of Cambodians, Chinese, "Montagnards" of several tribes, and other groups. Vietnam also is a land of diverse religions, with Buddhists, Catholics, Confucists, and a variety of other sects, some of which have until recently exercised temporal as well as spiritual power. Lastly, as a legacy of long-time foreign control, by China, France and Japan, Vietnam has little tradition or experience in democratic government. All of these factors, and the problems they generate, make the job of central government exceedingly difficult and cloud the basic issue at stake. That issue can be put several ways.

General Giap, commander of the North Vietnamese Army, has stated publicly: "South Vietnam is the model of the national liberation movement of our time . . . If the special warfare that the United States imperialists are testing in South Vietnam is overcome, then it can be defeated everywhere in the world." I underline the word, "*everywhere.*"

Lin Piao, Communist Chinese Minister of Defense, set forth the issue in clearest detail in an 18,000-word manifesto which all Americans would profit by studying. It is a latter-day Mein Kampf. It leaves no room for doubt that he pictures a move from conquest of the so-called "rural areas"—Asia, Africa, and Latin America—to conquest of the so-called "cities of the world"—North America and Western Europe. With this in mind, Lin says that Vietnam is . . . "now the focus of the struggle of the people of the world against U.S. aggression."

On the other hand, as long ago as 1962, the Legal Committee of the International Control Commission, in Vietnam, issued a majority report, signed by India and Canada, which stated: ". . . there is evidence to show that armed and unarmed personnel, arms, munitions, and other supplies have been sent from the Zone in the North to the Zone in the South with the object of supporting, organizing, and carrying out the hostile activities, including armed attacks, directed against the Armed Forces and Administration of the Zone of the South. These acts, they reported, "are in violation of Articles 10, 19, 24 and 27 of the Agreement on the Cessation of Hostilities in Vietnam."[7]

In the years which have followed, the South Vietnamese and we have had overwhelming evidence that the basic issue in that land is indeed one of outright, external, communist aggression. Let me list, most briefly, just some of the facts which lead to this conclusion:

First, when the Viet Minh supposedly withdrew north in 1954, we know that they left behind a military and political cadre to organize resistance. Subsequently, many more Southerners who had moved north for training and indoctrination were infiltrated back into the south to reinforce these cadres.

Second, we note the public statements and propaganda of Hanoi and Peiping themselves, to include the announcement in 1960, from Hanoi—*not* from South Vietnam—of the formation of the so-called "Front for Liberation of the South."

Third, we observe the strangely faceless and alien character of the supposedly indigenous Viet Cong. The heroes of the enemy are Ho Chi Minh and General Giap, not South Vietnamese. The Viet Cong leaders are nearly unknown. In South Vietnam, no single, well-known leader since partition—regardless of internal differences—has supported the Viet Cong.

Fourth, we have seen the Viet Cong employ unrestrained

[7] Assess the quality of the evidence in the three preceding paragraphs. What is the purpose of these quotations?

terror against the men, women and children of a land which, in theory, they are defending against so-called "aggression." In 1964 and 1965 alone, more than 2100 South Vietnamese officials were murdered or kidnapped. In a nation that size, that is the equivalent of 27,000 murders and kidnappings in the United States. Beyond these officials, nearly 22,000 other Vietnamese civilians were murdered or taken away. In equivalent American terms—more than 280,000 people.[8]

Fifth, we have the constantly mounting evidence of arms and ammunition supplied from North Vietnam, China, and other communist nations.

Sixth, we have proof of every sort of massive, organized land and sea infiltration from the north. Several regular North Vietnamese divisions have invaded South Vietnam, and the hard core Viet Cong units are relying increasingly on North Vietnamese replacements. With this in mind, I have often wondered:

If many thousands of armed South Korean were to penetrate North Korea and wage a war directed from Seoul, what would the communists call this—a revolution, or aggression?

If many thousands of armed West Germans were to penetrate East Germany and wage a war directed from Bonn, what would the communists call this—a revolution, or aggression?

The list could go on, but those examples are illustrative of the basic issue confronted by South Vietnam—aggression. U. Alexis Johnson, now our ambassador to Japan and a distinguished diplomat of wide Asian experience, recently put it this way:

"The question is not whether Vietnam itself, or indeed Southeast Asia as a whole, is of such political, strategic, or economic importance as to justify asking our men and women to risk their lives there.

"Rather," he said, "the question is the world-wide effect of permitting the Communists to breach by force any of the lines that were drawn in the various post-war settlements. The 17th parallel in Vietnam is just as much a part of those settlements

[8] Why does this point receive greater development than the other five?

as Checkpoint Charlie, the 38th parallel, or the northern border of Greece . . .

"The principle of self-determination is paramount . . . Will countries be permitted to develop their own way without outside interference? Or shall we merely watch as they are subjected to infiltration, invasion, and terrorism . . . ?"

I agree that that is the issue, and I would also point out that a precious commodity is at stake as far as we are concerned—the integrity of our word.[9]

In this crowded, smaller, and more dangerous world, we are all, as John Donne said, "involved in Mankind." And, if we are not involved for altruistic reasons, we are involved for the simplest of practical reasons: in this small world we cannot escape involvement. While fortune has made us the richest and the strongest of nations, no country can stand alone. For reasons of self interest as well as principle, then, we have allied ourselves with those nations which believe in individual freedom and national independence. As the leader of the community of free men, we have committed our word to the defense of freedom.

We might have been called upon to honor our commitment in any one of several places. The challenge came in Vietnam.

In sum, what I have said to you tonight can be expressed in a paraphrase of Benjamin Franklin's words to his colleagues of the Continental Congress on the occasion of the signing of the Declaration of Independence: If the free nations of the world do not hang together in opposing aggression, then surely they will hang separately.

CRITICAL ANALYSIS AND PROJECTS

1. After devoting approximately one-third of his speech to a bland discussion of how world conditions have changed in recent years, Wheeler offers his thesis that Vietnam is an extension of a struggle "which has

[9] Evaluate Wheeler's use of the argument that the United States' involvement in Vietnam has resulted from a decision to honor a commitment to the Vietnamese government.

been imposed upon the free peoples for twenty years." Why did he choose this pattern of organization? Can you suggest a better one?

2. Except for the first six paragraphs, what internal evidence is there that this speech was prepared specifically for the Brown University audience?
3. Wheeler says that the United States government has "overwhelming evidence that the basic issue in that [Vietnam] land is indeed one of outright, external Communist aggression." What specific evidence does he offer to support this point in his speech?
4. What evidence is there in his speech that Wheeler understands the people and military powers in Southeast Asia?
5. What issues might Wheeler have discussed to make the speech of more interest to college students?
6. A military-industrial complex is often accused of unduly influencing American foreign policy. Investigate this charge and report your findings in a speech to the class. See items 2. and 5. in the bibliography.
7. In light of contemporary events, prepare a speech in which you describe the military or foreign policy lessons to be learned from the Vietnam conflict.

SELECTED BIBLIOGRAPHY

1. Armbruster, Frank E., *et al. Can We Win in Vietnam?* New York: Frederick A. Praeger, 1968.
2. Coffin, Tristram. *The Armed Society: Militarism in Modern America.* Baltimore: Penguin Books, 1964.
3. Fall, Bernard B., ed. *Ho-Chi-Minh on Revolution: Selected Writings, 1920–1966.* New York: Frederick A. Praeger, 1967.
4. "Heir Apparent," *Newsweek,* LIX (March 5, 1962), 36.
5. Herzog, Arthur. *The War-Peace Establishment.* New York: Harper and Row, 1965.
6. Janowitz, Morris. *The Professional Soldier: A Social and Political Portrait.* Glencoe, Ill.: Free Press, 1960.
7. Knorr, Klaus. *On the Uses of Military Power in the Nuclear Age.* Princeton, N.J.: Princeton University Press, 1966.
8. "Merit Will be Rewarded," *Newsweek,* LXIV (July 6, 1964), 19.
9. Molnar, Thomas. *The Two Faces of American Foreign Policy.* Indianapolis: Bobbs-Merrill, 1962.
10. Swomley, John M. *The Military Establishment.* Boston: Beacon Press, 1964.

PART FIVE

DISSENT AND VIETNAM

IX

J. WILLIAM FULBRIGHT

The Price of Empire

On March 25, 1964, Senator J. William Fulbright stood before a nearly-empty Senate chamber and took another bold step toward building bridges between the East and West. In his speech labeled "Old Myths and New Realities," he denounced the stereotypes and fears that had long filled American speeches on foreign policy and called for the acknowledgment that the Soviet Union, "though still a most formidable adversary, has ceased to be totally and implacably hostile to the West."[1]

Although the speech was widely criticized, it did not represent a departure from the boldness that Senator Fulbright had followed during his one term in the House and four terms in the Senate. In 1943 he sponsored the Fulbright Resolution, which led the transfer of American opinion away from isolationism. He cast the lone dissenting vote in the Senate against additional funds for the Special Investigating Subcommittee chaired in 1954 by the late Senator Joseph McCarthy. In 1959 the Senator from Arkansas became chairman of the Senate Committee on Foreign Relations, the position he occupied when he launched a full-scale investigation in February 1966, of the Johnson administration's Vietnam policy.

Reprinted from *Congressional Record,* 90th Cong., 1st Sess. (August 9, 1967), 11265–11268, by permission of J. William Fulbright.

[1] J. William Fulbright, *Old Myths and New Realities* (New York: Random House, 1964), p. 9.

During the summer of 1967 the United States was badly scarred by rioting and shootings in several of its cities and by increased dissension over the Vietnam war. Senator Fulbright relates both of these problems to American foreign policy in his speech at a luncheon during the American Bar Association Convention in Honolulu on August 9, 1967.

Standing in the smoke and rubble of Detroit, a Negro veteran said: "I just got back from Vietnam a few months ago, but you know, I think the war is here."

There are in fact two wars going on. One is the war of power politics which our soldiers are fighting in the jungles of southeast Asia. The other is a war for America's soul which is being fought in the streets of Newark and Detroit and in the halls of Congress, in churches and protest meetings and on college campuses, and in the hearts and minds of silent Americans from Maine to Hawaii. I believe that the two wars have something to do with each other, not in the direct, tangibly causal way that bureaucrats require as proof of a connection between two things, but in a subtler, moral and qualitative way that is no less real for being intangible. Each of these wars might well be going on in the absence of the other, but neither, I suspect, standing alone, would seem so hopeless and demoralizing.

The connection between Vietnam and Detroit is in their conflicting and incompatible demands upon traditional American values. The one demands that they be set aside, the other that they be fulfilled. The one demands the acceptance by America of an imperial role in the world, or of what our policy makers like to call the "responsibilities of power," or of what I have called the "arrogance of power." The other demands freedom and social justice at home, an end to poverty, the fulfillment of our flawed democracy, and an effort to create a role for ourselves in the world which is compatible with our traditional values.[2] The question, it should be

[2] What special technique is Fulbright using to heighten the conflict between conditions in Vietnam and in American cities?

emphasized, is not whether it is *possible* to engage in traditional power politics abroad and at the same time to perfect democracy at home, but whether it is possible for *us Americans,* with our particular history and national character, to combine morally incompatible roles.

Administration officials tell us that we can indeed afford both Vietnam and the Great Society, and they produce impressive statistics of the gross national product to prove it. The statistics show financial capacity but they do not show moral and psychological capacity. They do not show how a President preoccupied with bombing missions over North and South Vietnam can provide strong and consistent leadership for the renewal of our cities. They do not show how a Congress burdened with war costs and war measures, with emergency briefings and an endless series of dramatic appeals, with anxious constituents and a mounting anxiety of their own, can tend to the workaday business of studying social problems and legislating programs to meet them. Nor do the statistics tell how an anxious and puzzled people, bombarded by press and television with the bad news of American deaths in Vietnam, the "good news" of enemy deaths—and with vividly horrifying pictures to illustrate them—can be expected to support neighborhood anti-poverty projects and national programs for urban renewal, employment and education. Anxiety about war does not breed compassion for one's neighbors; nor do constant reminders of the cheapness of life abroad strengthen our faith in its sanctity at home. In these ways the war in Vietnam is poisoning and brutalizing our domestic life. Psychological incompatibility has proven to be more controlling than financial feasibility; and the Great Society has become a sick society.[3]

When he visited America a hundred years ago, Thomas Huxley wrote: "I cannot say that I am in the slightest degree impressed by your bigness, or your material resources, as such. Size is not grandeur, and territory does not make a nation. The great issue, about which hangs the terror of overhanging fate, is what are you going to do with all these things?"

[3] What method of argument does he use to refute statistical claims without using statistics?

The question is still with us and we seem to have come to a time of historical crisis when its answer can no longer be deferred. Before the Second World War our world role was a *potential* role; we were important in the world for what we *could* do with our power, for the leadership we *might* provide, for the example we *might* set. Now the choices are almost gone: we are *almost* the world's self-appointed policeman; we are *almost* the world defender of the *status quo*. We are well on our way to becoming a traditional great power—an imperial nation if you will—engaged in the exercise of power for its own sake, exercising it to the limit of our capacity and beyond, filling every vacuum and extending the American "presence" to the farthest reaches of the earth. And, as with the great empires of the past, as the power grows, it is becoming an end in itself, separated except by ritual incantation from its initial motives, governed, it would seem, by its own mystique, power without philosophy or purpose.

That describes what we have *almost* become, but we have not become a traditional empire yet. The old values remain—the populism and the optimism, the individualism and the rough-hewn equality, the friendliness and the good humor, the inventiveness and the zest for life, the caring about people and the sympathy for the underdog, and the idea, which goes back to the American Revolution, that maybe—just maybe—we can set an example of democracy and human dignity for the world.[4]

That is something which none of the great empires of the past has ever done—or tried to do—or wanted to do—but we were bold enough—or presumptuous enough—to think that we might be able to do it. And there are a great many Americans who still think we can do it—or at least they want to try.

That, I believe, is what all the hue and cry is about—the dissent in the Senate and the protest marches in the cities, the letters to the President from student leaders and former Peace Corps volunteers, the lonely searching of conscience by a

[4] Classify the appeals in this paragraph. Why are they likely to evoke a response from his audience?

student facing the draft and the letter to a Senator from a soldier in the field who can no longer accept the official explanations of why he has been sent to fight in the jungles of Vietnam. All believe that their country was cut out for something more ennobling than an imperial destiny. Our youth are showing that they still believe in the American dream, and their protests attest to its continuing vitality.

There appeared in a recent issue of the journal *Foreign Affairs* a curious little article complaining about the failure of many American intellectuals to support what the author regards as America's unavoidable "imperial role" in the world. The article took my attention because it seems a faithful statement of the governing philosophy of American foreign policy while also suggesting how little the makers of that policy appreciate the significance of the issue between themselves and their critics. It is taken for granted—not set forth as an hypothesis to be proved—that, any great power, in the author's words, "is entangled in a web of responsibilities from which there is no hope of escape," and that "there is no way the United States, as the world's mightiest power, can avoid such an imperial role. . . ."[5] The author's displeasure with the "intellectuals"—he uses the word more or less to describe people who disagree with the Administration's policy—is that, in the face of this alleged historical inevitability, they are putting up a disruptive, irritating and futile resistance. They are doing this, he believes, because they are believers in "ideology"—the better word would be "values" or "ideals"—and this causes their thinking to be "irrelevant" to foreign policy.

Here, inadvertently, the writer puts his finger on the nub of the current crisis. The students and churchmen and professors who are protesting the Vietnam war do not accept the notion that foreign policy is a matter of expedients to which values are irrelevant. They reject this notion because they understand, as some of our policy makers do not understand, that it is ultimately self-defeating to "fight fire with fire," that you

[5] Irving Kristol, "American Intellectuals and Foreign Policy," *Foreign Affairs* (July 1967), pp. 602, 605. [J. W. F.]

cannot defend your values in a manner that does violence to those values without destroying the very thing you are trying to defend. They understand, as our policy makers do not, that when American soldiers are sent, in the name of freedom, to sustain corrupt dictators in a civil war, that when the CIA subverts student organizations to engage in propaganda activities abroad, or when the Export-Import Bank is used by the Pentagon to finance secret arms sales abroad, damage—perhaps irreparable damage—is being done to the very values that are meant to be defended. The critics understand, as our policy makers do not, that, through the undemocratic expedients we have adopted for the defense of American democracy, we are weakening it to a degree that is beyond the resources of our bitterest enemies.[6]

Nor do the dissenters accept the romantic view that a nation is powerless to choose the role it will play in the world, that some mystic force of history or destiny requires a powerful nation to be an imperial nation, dedicated to what Paul Goodman calls the "empty system of power,"[7] to the pursuit of power without purpose, philosophy or compassion. They do not accept the Hegelian concept of history as something out of control, as something that happens to us rather than something that we make. They do not accept the view that, because other great nations have pursued power for its own sake—a pursuit which invariably has ended in decline or disaster—America must do the same. They think we have some choice about our own future and that the best basis for exercising that choice is the values on which this republic was founded.

The critics of our current course also challenge the contention that the traditional methods of foreign policy are safe and prudent and realistic. They are understandably skeptical of their wise and experienced elders who, in the name of prudence, caution against any departure from the tried and true

[6] What persuasive advantage is there in Fulbright's decision to let the dissenters express his viewpoint rather than make explicit statements of his own?

[7] *Like a Conquered Province: The Moral Ambiguity of America* (New York: Random House, 1967), p. 73. [J. W. F.]

methods that have led in this century to Sarajevo, Munich and Dien Bien Phu. They think that the methods of the past have been tried and found wanting, and two world wars attest powerfully to their belief. Most of all, they think that, in this first era of human history in which man has acquired weapons which threaten his entire species with destruction, safety and prudence and realism require us to change the rules of a dangerous and discredited game, to try as we have never tried before to civilize and humanize international relations, not only for the sake of civilization and humanity but for the sake of survival.

Even the most ardent advocates of an imperial role for the United States would probably agree that the proper objective of our foreign policy is the fostering of a world environment in which we can, with reasonable security, devote our main energies to the realization of the values of our own society. This does not require the adoption or imposition of these values on anybody, but it does require us so to conduct ourselves that our society does not seem hateful and repugnant to others.

At present much of the world is repelled by America and what America seems to stand for in the world. Both in our foreign affairs and in our domestic life we convey an image of violence; I do not care very much about images as distinguished from the things they reflect, but this image is rooted in reality. Abroad we are engaged in a savage and unsuccessful war against poor people in a small and backward nation. At home—largely because of the neglect resulting from twenty-five years of preoccupation with foreign involvements—our cities are exploding in violent protest against generations of social injustice. America, which only a few years ago seemed to the world to be a model of democracy and social justice, has become a symbol of violence and undisciplined power.

". . . it is excellent," wrote Shakespeare, "to have a giant's strength; but it is tyrannous to use it like a giant."[8] By using our power like a giant we are fostering a world environment which is, to put it mildly, uncongenial to our society. By our

[8] *Measure for Measure,* Act II, Scene 2, Line 107. [J. W. F.]

undisciplined use of physical power we have divested ourselves of a greater power: the power of example. How, for example, can we commend peaceful compromise to the Arabs and the Israelis when we are unwilling to suspend our relentless bombing of North Vietnam? How can we commend democratic social reform to Latin America when Newark, Detroit, and Milwaukee are providing explosive evidence of our own inadequate efforts at democratic social reform? How can we commend the free enterprise system to Asians and Africans when in our own country it has produced vast, chaotic, noisy, dangerous and dirty urban complexes while poisoning the very air and land and water?[9] There may come a time when Americans will again be able to commend their country as an example to the world and, more in hope than confidence, I retain my faith that there will; but to do so right at this moment would take more gall than I have.

Far from building a safe world environment for American values, our war in Vietnam and the domestic deterioration which it has aggravated are creating a most uncongenial world atmosphere for American ideas and values. The world has no need, in this age of nationalism and nuclear weapons, for a new imperial power, but there is a great need of moral leadership—by which I mean the leadership of decent example. That role could be ours but we have vacated the field, and all that has kept the Russians from filling it is their own lack of imagination.

At the same time, as we have noted, and of even greater fundamental importance, our purposeless and undisciplined use of power is causing a profound controversy in our own society. This in a way is something to be proud of. We have sickened but not succumbed and just as a healthy body fights disease, we are fighting the alien concept which is being thrust upon us, not by history but by our policy makers in the Department of State and the Pentagon. We are proving the strength of the American dream by resisting the dream of an imperial destiny. We are demonstrating the validity of our

[9] Assess Fulbright's use of rhetorical questions to show the damage to America's leadership abilities.

traditional values by the difficulty we are having in betraying them.

The principal defenders of these values are our remarkable younger generation, something of whose spirit is expressed in a letter which I received from an American soldier in Vietnam. Speaking of the phony propaganda on both sides, and then of the savagery of the war, or the people he describes as the "real casualties"—"the farmers and their families in the Delta mangled by air strikes, and the villagers here killed and burned out by our friendly Korean mercenaries"—this young soldier then asks ". . . whatever has become of our dream? Where is that America that opposed tyrannies at every turn, without inquiring first whether some particular forms of tyranny might be of use to us? Of the three rights which men have, the first, as I recall, was the right to life. How then have we come to be killing so many in such a dubious cause?"[10]

While the death toll mounts in Vietnam, it is mounting too in the war at home. During a single week of July 1967, 164 Americans were killed and 1,442 wounded in Vietnam, while 65 Americans were killed and 2,100 were wounded in city riots in the United States. We are truly fighting a two-front war and doing badly in both. Each war feeds on the other and, although the President assures us that we have the resources to win both wars, in fact we are not winning either.

Together the two wars have set in motion a process of deterioration in American society and there is no question that each of the two crises is heightened by the impact of the other. Not only does the Vietnam war divert human and material resources from our festering cities; not only does it foster the conviction on the part of slum Negroes that their country is indifferent to their plight. In addition the war feeds the idea of violence as a way of solving problems. If, as Mr. Rusk tells us, only the rain of bombs can bring Ho Chi Minh to reason, why should not the same principle apply at home? Why should not riots and snipers' bullets bring the white man

[10] What is the impact of the soldier's letter upon the tone of the speech?

to an awareness of the Negro's plight when peaceful programs for housing and jobs and training have been more rhetoric than reality? Ugly and shocking thoughts are in the American air and they were forged in the Vietnam crucible. Black power extremists talk of "wars of liberation" in the urban ghettoes of America. A cartoon in a London newspaper showed two Negro soldiers in battle in Vietnam with one saying to the other: "This is going to be great training for civilian life."

The effect of domestic violence on the chances for peace in Vietnam may turn out to be no less damaging than the impact of the war on events at home. With their limited knowledge of the United States, the Vietcong and the North Vietnamese may regard the urban riots as a harbinger of impending breakdown and eventual American withdrawal from Vietnam, warranting stepped up warfare and an uncompromising position on negotiations. It is possible that the several opportunities to negotiate which our government has let pass, most recently last winter, could not now be retrieved. Some eighteen months ago General Maxwell Taylor said in testimony before the Senate Foreign Relations Committee that the war was being prolonged by domestic dissent. That dissent was based in part on apprehension as to the effects of the war on our domestic life. Now the war is being prolonged by the domestic deterioration which has in fact occurred and it is doubtful that all of the dissenters in America, even if they wanted to, as they certainly do not, could give the enemy a fraction of the aid and comfort that has been given him by Newark, Detroit and Milwaukee.

An unnecessary and immoral war deserves in its own right to be liquidated; when its effect in addition is the aggravation of grave problems and the corrosion of values in our own society, its liquidation under terms of reasonable and honorable compromise is doubly imperative. Our country is being weakened by a grotesque inversion of priorities, the effects of which are becoming clear to more and more Americans—in the Congress, in the press and in the country at large. Even the *Washington Post,* a newspaper which has obsequiously supported the Administration's policy in Vietnam, took note in a recent editorial of the "ugly image of a world policeman incapable of policing itself" as against the "absolute necessity of a sound domestic base for an effective foreign policy," and then commented: "We are confronted simultaneously with an urgent domestic crisis and an urgent foreign crisis and our commitments to both are clear. We should deal with both with all the energy and time and resources that may be required. But if the moment ever arises when we cannot deal adequately and effectively with both, there is no shame—and some considerable logic—in making it plain beyond a doubt that our first consideration and our first priority rests with the security of the stockade."[11]

Commenting on the same problem of priorities, Mayor Cavanaugh of Detroit said:

"What will it profit this country if we, say, put our man on the moon by 1970 and at the same time you can't walk down Woodward Avenue in this city without some fear of violence?

"And we may be able to pacify every village in Vietnam, over a period of years, but what good does it do if we can't pacify the American cities?

"What I am saying . . . is that our priorities in this country are all out of balance . . . Maybe Detroit was a watershed this week in American history and it might well be that out of the ashes of this city comes the national resolve to do far more than anything we have done in the past."[12]

Priorities are reflected in the things we spend money on. Far from being a dry accounting of bookkeepers, a nation's budget is full of moral implications; it tells what a society cares about and what it does not care about; it tells what its values are.

Here are a few statistics on America's values: Since 1946 we have spent over $1,578 billion through our regular national budget. Of this amount over $904 billion, or 57.29 percent of the total, have gone for military power. By contrast, less than $96 billion, or 6.08 percent, were spent on "social functions" including education, health, labor and welfare programs, housing and community development. The Administration's bud-

[11] *The Washington Post,* July 27, 1967. [J. W. F.]

[12] Comments on "Meet the Press," reported in *The Washington Post,* July 31, 1967. [J. W. F.]

get for fiscal year 1968 calls for almost $76 billion to be spent on the military and only $15 billion for "social functions."

I would not say that we have shown ourselves to value weapons five or ten times as much as we value domestic social needs, as the figures suggest; certainly much of our military spending has been necessitated by genuine requirements of national security. I think, however, that we have embraced the necessity with excessive enthusiasm, that the Congress has been all too willing to provide unlimited sums for the military and not really very reluctant at all to offset these costs to a very small degree by cutting away funds for the poverty program and urban renewal, for rent supplements for the poor and even for a program to help protect slum children from being bitten by rats. Twenty million dollars a year to eliminate rats—about one one-hundredth of the monthly cost of the war in Vietnam—would not eliminate slum riots but, as Tom Wicker has written, "It would only suggest that somebody cared."[13] The discrepancy of attitudes tells at least as much about our national values as the discrepancy of dollars.[14]

While the country sickens for lack of moral leadership, a most remarkable younger generation has taken up the standard of American idealism. Unlike so many of their elders, they have perceived the fraud and sham in American life and are unequivocally rejecting it. Some, the hippies, have simply withdrawn, and while we may regret the loss of their energies and their sense of decency, we can hardly gainsay their evaluation of the state of society. Others of our youth are sardonic and skeptical, not, I think, because they do not want ideals but because they want the genuine article and will not tolerate fraud. Others—students who wrestle with their consciences about the draft, soldiers who wrestle with their consciences about the war, Peace Corps volunteers who strive to light the spark of human dignity among the poor of India or Brazil, and VISTA volunteers who try to do the same for our

[13] *The New York Times,* July 23, 1967. [J. W. F.]

[14] Evaluate Fulbright's use of statistics to show national attitudes. How does he make the figures meaningful for his audience?

own poor in Harlem or Appalachia—are striving to keep alive the traditional values of American democracy.

They are not really radical, these young idealists, no more radical, that is, than Jefferson's idea of freedom, Lincoln's idea of equality, or Wilson's idea of a peaceful community of nations. Some of them, it is true, are taking what many regard as radical action, but they are doing it in defense of traditional values and in protest against the radical departure from those values embodied in the idea of an imperial destiny for America.

The focus of their protest is the war in Vietnam and the measure of their integrity is the fortitude with which they refused to be deceived about it. By striking contrast with the young Germans who accepted the Nazi evil because the values of their society had disintegrated and they had no normal frame of reference, these young Americans are demonstrating the vitality of American values. They are demonstrating that, while their country is capable of acting falsely to itself, it cannot do so without internal disruption, without calling forth the regenerative counterforce of protest from Americans who are willing to act in defense of the principles they were brought up to believe in.

The spirit of this regenerative generation has been richly demonstrated to me in letters from student leaders, from former Peace Corps volunteers and from soldiers fighting in Vietnam. I quoted from one earlier in my remarks. Another letter that is both striking and representative was written by an officer still in Vietnam. He wrote:

"For eleven years I was, before this war, a Regular commissioned officer—a professional military man in name and spirit; now—in name only. To fight well (as do the VC), a soldier must believe in his leadership. I, and many I have met, have lost faith in ours. Since I hold that duty to conscience is higher than duty to the administration (not 'country' as cry the nationalists), I declined a promotion and have resigned my commission. I am to be discharged on my return, at which time I hope to contribute in some way to the search for peace in Vietnam."

Some years ago Archibald MacLeish characterized the American people as follows:

"Races didn't bother the Americans. They were something a lot better than any race. They were a People. They were the first self-constituted, self-declared, self-created People in the history of the world. And their manners were their own business. And so were their politics. And so, but ten times so, were their souls."[15]

Now the possession of their souls is being challenged by the false and dangerous dream of an imperial destiny. It may be that the challenge will succeed, that America will succumb to becoming a traditional empire and will reign for a time over what must surely be a moral if not a physical wasteland, and then, like the great empires of the past, will decline or fall. Or it may be that the effort to create so grotesque an anachronism will go up in flames of nuclear holocaust. But if I had to bet my money on what is going to happen. I would bet on this younger generation—this generation who reject the inhumanity of war in a poor and distant land, who reject the poverty and sham in their own country, this generation who are telling their elders what their elders ought to have known, that the price of empire is America's soul and that price is too high.[16]

CRITICAL ANALYSIS AND PROJECTS

1. What is Fulbright's thesis and what are his main arguments in support of it?
2. In several segments of the speech the forcefulness comes from Fulbright's selection of powerful verbs. Underline all the sentences that have strong verbs and determine their role in advancing the speaker's main points.

[15] Archibald MacLeish, *A Time To Act* (Boston: Houghton Mifflin Co., 1943), p. 115. [J. W. F.]

[16] Fulbright chooses not to offer a solution to the Vietnam war but praises instead the insights of America's youth. Why doesn't he offer a solution?

3. Why is Fulbright's defense of dissenters an important part of his speech?
4. Compile a list of the rhetorical figures he uses. Compare his use of stylistic devices with those found in Goldwater's speech. Which speaker has the more effective style?
5. Read Fulbright's speech on "The Arrogance of Power" or "Old Myths and New Realities." What are the major arguments against current American foreign policy?
6. Fulbright charges America with having an image of violence in the court of world opinion. Prepare a speech in which you describe one step America should take to change this impression.
7. Prepare a speech in which you attack or defend Fulbright's belief that America is practicing an "arrogance of power" in its foreign policy.

SELECTED BIBLIOGRAPHY

1. Ball, George. "The Dangers of Nostalgia," *Department of State Bulletin,* LII (April 12, 1965), 532–537.
2. Coffin, Tristram. *Senator Fulbright: Portrait of a Public Philosopher.* New York: E. P. Dutton, 1966.
3. Fulbright, J. William. *The Arrogance of Power.* New York: Random House, 1966.
4. ———. *Prospects for the West.* Cambridge, Mass.: Harvard University Press, 1963.
5. ———. *The Two Americas.* Storrs, Conn.: University of Connecticut Press, 1966.
6. Kelly, Lera Rowlette. "The Speaking of J. William Fulbright," *Southern Speech Journal,* XXVII (Spring 1962), 232–238.
7. McCarthy, Eugene J. *The Limits of Power.* New York: Holt, Rinehart and Winston, 1967.
8. Meyer, Karl E., ed. *Fulbright of Arkansas.* Washington, D.C.: Robert B. Luce, 1963.
9. Steel, Ronald. *Pax Americana.* New York: The Viking Press, 1967.
10. Toynbee, Arnold J. *War and Civilization.* Albert V. Fowler, ed. New York: Oxford University Press, 1950.
11. *The Vietnam Hearings.* New York: Random House, 1966.
12. Wright, Quincy, William M. Evan, and Morton Deutsch, eds. *Preventing World War III: Some Proposals.* New York: Simon and Schuster, 1962.

X

LYNDON B. JOHNSON

A New Step Toward Peace

Lyndon B. Johnson became the thirty-sixth president of the United States on November 22, 1963, following the assassination of President John F. Kennedy. Five days later he made his first policy speech before a joint session of Congress and a nationwide television audience. After announcing his full support of Kennedy's legislative programs, the President promised to keep the nation militarily strong while pursuing avenues to peace. In 1964 Mr. Johnson became the Democratic party's candidate for president and won a landslide victory over Senator Barry Goldwater.

President Johnson's overwhelming popularity, however, did not last. The Vietnam crisis, which he had inherited from the Kennedy administration, produced increasing divisiveness among the American people and within his own party. Despite his efforts to end the war, he saw his popularity fall until in late March 1968, a Gallup Poll showed that only 36 percent of the Americans polled approved of his handling of the presidency and only 26 percent supported his actions in Vietnam.[1]

Senator Eugene McCarthy's primary victory in New Hampshire strengthened his bid for the Democratic presidential nomination and further underscored Democratic dissatisfaction with President Johnson. Shortly after Senator McCarthy's New Hampshire victory, Senator Robert Kennedy also announced he would seek the Democratic nomination.

From a transcription of the speech as broadcast by CBS television, April 15, 1968.

[1] *The New York Times,* April 1, 1968.

Meanwhile, President Johnson continued to look for a negotiated peace in Vietnam and announced that he would make a major address to the nation on March 31, 1968. In his speech he announced the immediate cessation of bombing over "almost 90 percent of North Vietnam's population and most of its territory" and called for President Ho Chi Minh to send delegates for peace negotiations. Although the speech called for a change in tactics, it indicated no fundamental changes in American policy. The surprise came in the peroration.

Rumors had circulated for nearly a year that President Johnson might not run for reelection, but they were quickly dismissed. According to the President, however, he reached his decision in November 1967, during General William Westmoreland's visit to Washington.[2] Press Secretary George Christian reported drafting in December a "contingency statement" disclosing the decision not to seek reelection. This was the first of several drafts distilled by the President into his March 31 announcement. He apparently had one draft of the announcement with him when he delivered the State of the Union address in January 1968.[3]

President Johnson's speeches were seldom praised because of his "funeral voice" and lack-lustre style, but his address of March 31 was one of his best. If the Paris negotiations bring peace in Vietnam, this speech will become a landmark in American history.

Good evening, my fellow Americans. Tonight I want to speak to you of peace in Vietnam and Southeast Asia. No other question so preoccupies our people. No other dream so absorbs the 250 million human beings who live in that part of the world. No other goal motivates American policy in Southeast Asia.[4]

[2] *Ibid.*

[3] *Ibid.*

[4] Determine the effectiveness of the negative statements used in this paragraph.

For years, representatives of our government and others have traveled the world seeking to find a basis for peace talks. Since last September they have carried the offer that I made public at San Antonio. And that offer was this:

That the United States would stop its bombardment of North Vietnam when that would lead promptly to productive discussions—and that we would assume that North Vietnam would not take military advantage of our restraint.

Hanoi denounced this offer, both privately and publicly. Even while the search for peace was going on, North Vietnam rushed their preparations for a savage assault on the people, the government, and the allies of South Vietnam.

Their attack—during the Tet holidays—failed to achieve its principal objective. It did not collapse the elected government of South Vietnam or shatter its army—as the Communists had hoped. It did not produce a "general uprising" among the people of the cities as they had predicted.

The Communists were unable to maintain control of any of the more than thirty cities that they attacked, and they took very heavy casualties. But they did compel the South Vietnamese and their allies to move certain forces from the countryside into the cities. They caused widespread disruption and suffering. Their attacks, and the battles that followed, made refugees of half a million human beings.

The Communists may renew their attack any day. They are, it appears, trying to make 1968 the year of decision in South Vietnam—the year that brings, if not final victory or defeat, at least a turning point in the struggle.

This much is clear: If they do mount another round of heavy attacks, they will not succeed in destroying the fighting power of South Vietnam and its allies.

But tragically, this is also clear: many men—on both sides of the struggle—will be lost. A nation that has already suffered twenty years of warfare will suffer once again. Armies on both sides will take new casualties. And the war will go on.

There is no need for this to be so. There is no need to delay the talks that could bring an end to this long and this bloody war. Tonight I renew the offer I made last August—to stop the bombardment of North Vietnam. We ask that talks begin promptly, that they be serious talks on the substance of peace. We assume that during those talks Hanoi will not take advantage of our restraint. We are prepared to move immediately toward peace through negotiations. So, tonight, in the hope that this action will lead to early talks, I am taking the first step to de-escalate the conflict. We are reducing—substantially reducing—the present level of hostilities. And we are doing so unilaterally, and at once.

Tonight I have ordered our aircraft and our naval vessels to make no attacks on North Vietnam, except in the area north of the Demilitarized Zone where the continuing enemy buildup directly threatens allied forward positions and where the movements of their troops and supplies are clearly related to that threat. The area in which we are stopping our attacks includes almost 90 percent of North Vietnam's population, and most of its territory. Thus there will be no attacks around the principal populated areas, or in the food-producing areas of North Vietnam. Even this very limited bombing of the North could come to an early end—if our restraint is matched by restraint in Hanoi. But I cannot in good conscience stop all bombing so long as to do so would immediately and directly endanger the lives of our men and our allies. Whether a complete bombing halt becomes possible in the future will be determined by events.

Our purpose in this action is to bring about a reduction in the level of violence that now exists. It is to save the lives of brave men—and to save the lives of innocent women and children. It is to permit the contending forces to move closer to a political settlement.[5]

And tonight I call upon the United Kingdom and I call upon the Soviet Union—as co-chairman of the Geneva Conferences, and as permanent members of the United Nations Security Council—to do all they can to move from the unilateral act of de-escalation that I have just announced toward genuine peace in Southeast Asia.

Now, as in the past, the United States is ready to send its

[5] What arguments does the President offer for ordering an immediate reduction in bombing?

representatives to any forum, at any time, to discuss the means of bringing this ugly war to an end. I am designating one of our most distinguished Americans, Ambassador Averell Harriman, as my personal representative for such talks. In addition, I have asked Ambassador Llewellyn Thompson, who returned from Moscow for consultation, to be available to join Ambassador Harriman at Geneva or any other suitable place—just as soon as Hanoi agrees to a conference.

I call upon President Ho Chi Minh to respond positively, and favorably, to this new step toward peace. But if peace does not come now through negotiations, it will come when Hanoi understands that our common resolve is unshakable, and our common strength is invincible.[6]

Tonight we and the other allied nations are contributing 600,000 fighting men to assist 700,000 South Vietnamese troops in defending their little country. Our presence there has always rested on this basic belief: the main burden of preserving their freedom must be carried out by them—by the South Vietnamese themselves. We and our allies can only help to provide a shield—behind which the people of South Vietnam can survive and can grow and develop. On their efforts—on their determinations and resourcefulness—the outcome will ultimately depend.

That small, beleagured nation has suffered terrible punishment for more than twenty years. I pay tribute once again tonight to the great courage and endurance of its people. South Vietnam supports armed forces tonight of almost 700,000 men—and I call your attention to the fact that that is the equivalent of more than 10 million in our own population. Its people maintain their firm determination to be free of domination by the North.[7]

There has been substantial progress, I think, in building a durable government during these last three years. The South Vietnam of 1965 could not have survived the enemy's Tet offensive of 1968. The elected government of South Vietnam

[6] What effect is this statement likely to have upon an enemy? Does it encourage conciliation?

[7] How does this paragraph relate to the President's overall strategy of reducing the American commitment in Vietnam?

survived that attack—and is rapidly repairing the devastation that it wrought.

The South Vietnamese know that further efforts are going to be required to expand their own armed forces; to move back into the countryside as quickly as possible; to increase their taxes; to select the very best men that they have for civil and military responsibility; to achieve a new unity within their constitutional government; and to include in the national effort all those groups who wish to preserve South Vietnam's control over its own destiny.

Last week President Thieu ordered the mobilization of 135,000 additional South Vietnamese. He plans to reach—as soon as possible—a total military strength of more than 800,000 men. To achieve this, the government of South Vietnam started the drafting of nineteen-year-olds on March 1. On May 1, the Government will begin the drafting of eighteen-year-olds. Last month, 10,000 men volunteered for military service. That was two and a half times the number of volunteers during the same month last year. Since the middle of January, more than 48,000 South Vietnamese have joined the armed forces and nearly half of them volunteered to do so. All men in the South Vietnamese armed forces have had their tours of duty extended for the duration of the war, and reserves are now being called up for immediate active duty.

President Thieu told his people last week, "We must make greater efforts. We must accept more sacrifices because, as I have said many times, this is our country. The existence of our nation is at stake, and this is mainly a Vietnamese responsibility."

He warned his people that a major national effort is required to root out corruption and incompetence at all levels of government. We applaud this evidence of determination on the part of South Vietnam. Our first priority will be to support their effort. We shall accelerate the re-equipment of South Vietnam's armed forces—in order to meet the enemy's increased firepower. This will enable them progressively to undertake a larger share of combat operations against the Communist invaders.[8]

[8] Why does the President devote so much of the speech to describing the military strength of Vietnam?

On many occasions I have told the American people that we would send to Vietnam those forces that are required to accomplish our mission there. So, with that as our guide, we have previously authorized a force level of approximately 525,000. Some weeks ago to help meet the enemy's new offensive we sent to Vietnam about 11,000 additional Marine and airborne troops. They were deployed by air in 48 hours on an emergency basis. But the artillery and the tank and aircraft and medical and other units that were needed to work with and support these infantry troops in combat could not then accompany them on that short notice.

In order that these forces may reach maximum combat effectiveness, the Joint Chiefs of Staff have recommended to me that we should prepare to send during the next five months support troops totaling approximately 13,500 men. A portion of these men will be made available from our active forces. The balance will come from reserve component units, which will be called up for service.

The actions that we have taken since the beginning of the year to re-equip the South Vietnamese forces; to meet our responsibilities in Korea, as well as our responsibilities in Vietnam; to meet price increases and the cost of activating and deploying these reserve forces; to replace helicopters and provide the other military supplies we need, all of these actions are going to require additional expenditures.

The tentative estimate of those additional expenditures is 2.5 billion dollars in this fiscal year, and 2.6 billion dollars in the next fiscal year. These projected increases will bring into sharper focus the nation's need for immediate action; action to protect the prosperity of the American people and to protect the strength and the stability of our American dollar.

On many occasions I have pointed out that, without a tax bill or decreased expenditures, next year's deficit would again be around $20 billion. I have emphasized the need to set strict priorities in our spending. I have stressed that failure to act and to act promptly and decisively would raise very strong doubt throughout the world about America's willingness to keep its financial house in order.

Yet Congress has not acted. And tonight we face the sharpest financial threat in the post-war era—a threat to the dollar's role as the keystone of international trade and finance in the world.

Last week, at the monetary conference in Stockholm the major industrial countries decided to take a big step toward creating a new international monetary asset that will strengthen the international monetary system. And, I'm very proud of the very able work done by Secretary Fowler and Chairman Martin of the Federal Reserve Board.

But to make this system work the United States just must bring its balance of payments to—or very close to—equilibrium. We must have a responsible fiscal policy in this country. The passage of a tax bill now, together with expenditure control that the Congress may desire and dictate, is absolutely necessary to protect this nation's security, to continue our prosperity, and to meet the needs of our people.

What is at stake is seven years of unparalleled prosperity. In those seven years, the real income of the average American after taxes rose by almost 30 percent—a gain as large as that of the entire preceding nineteen years.

So the steps that we must take to convince the world are exactly the steps we must take to sustain our own economic strength here at home. In the past eight months, prices and interest rates have risen because of our inaction. We must therefore, now do everything we can to move from debate to action, from talking to voting. There is, I believe—I hope there is—in both Houses of the Congress a growing sense of urgency that this situation just must be acted upon and must be corrected.

My budget in January was, we thought, a tight one. It fully reflected our evaluation of most of the demanding needs of this nation. But in these budgetary matters, the president does not decide alone. The Congress has the power and the duty to determine appropriations and taxes. The Congress is now considering our proposals and they are considering reductions in the budget that we submitted. As part of a program of fiscal restraint that includes the tax surcharge, I shall approve appropriate reductions in the January budget when and if Congress so decides that that should be done.

One thing is unmistakably clear, however. Our deficit just must be reduced. Failure to act could bring on conditions that would strike hardest at those people that all of us are trying so hard to help. These times call for prudence in this land of plenty. I believe that we have the character to provide it, and tonight I plead with the Congress and with the people to act promptly to serve the national interest and thereby serve all of our people.[9]

Now let me give you my estimate of the chances for peace—the peace that will one day stop the bloodshed in South Vietnam; so that all the Vietnamese people will be permitted to rebuild and develop their land; that will permit us to turn more fully to our own tasks here at home.

I cannot promise that the initiative that I have announced tonight will be completely successful in achieving peace any more than the thirty others that we have undertaken and agreed to in recent years. But it is our fervent hope that North Vietnam, after years of fighting that has left the issue unresolved, will now cease its efforts to achieve a military victory and will join with us in moving toward the peace table. And there may come a time when South Vietnamese—on both sides—are able to work out a way to settle their own differences by free political choice rather than by war.

As Hanoi considers its course, it should be in no doubt of our intentions. It must not miscalculate the pressures within our democracy in this election year. We have no intention of widening this war. But the United States will never accept a fake solution to this long and arduous struggle and call it peace.

No one can foretell the precise terms of an eventual settlement. Our objective in South Vietnam has never been the annihilation of the enemy. It has been to bring about a recognition in Hanoi that its objective—taking over the South by force—could not be achieved.

We think that peace can be based on the Geneva Accords of 1954—under political conditions that permit the South Vietnamese—all of the South Vietnamese—to chart their course free of any outside domination or interference, from us or

[9] What is the President's strongest argument for new tax legislation? How does he support it?

from anyone else. So tonight I reaffirm the pledge that we made at Manila—that we are prepared to withdraw our forces from South Vietnam as the other side withdraws its forces to the North, stops the infiltration, and the level of violence thus subsides.

Our goal of peace and self-determination in Vietnam is directly related to the future of all of Southeast Asia, where much has happened to inspire confidence during the past ten years. We have done all that we know how to do to contribute and to help build that confidence.

A number of its nations have shown what can be accomplished under conditions of security. Since 1966, Indonesia, the fifth largest nation in all the world, with a population of more than 100 million people, has had a government that is dedicated to peace with its neighbors and improved conditions for its own people. Political and economic cooperation between nations has grown rapidly.

And I think every American can take a great deal of pride in the role that we have played in bringing this about in Southeast Asia. We shall rightly judge—as responsible Southeast Asians themselves do—that the progress of the past three years would have been far less likely, if not completely impossible, if America's sons and others had not made their stand in Vietnam.

At Johns Hopkins University about three years ago, I announced that the United States would take part in the great work of developing Southeast Asia, including the Mekong Valley, for all the people of that region. Our determination to help build a better land—a better land for men on both sides of the present conflict—has not diminished in the least. Indeed, the ravages of war, I think, have made it more urgent than ever. So I repeat on behalf of the United States again tonight what I said at Johns Hopkins—that North Vietnam could take its place in this common effort just as soon as peace comes.

Over time, a wider framework of peace and security in Southeast Asia may become possible. The new cooperation of the nations in the area could be a foundation-stone. Certainly friendship with the nations of such as Southeast Asia is what the United States seeks—and that is all that the United States seeks.

One day, my fellow citizens, there will be peace in Southeast Asia. It will come because the people of Southeast Asia want it—those whose armies are at war tonight; those who, though threatened, have thus far been spared.

Peace will come because Asians were willing to work for it and to sacrifice for it—and to die by the thousands for it.

But let it never be forgotten: peace will come also because America sent her sons to help secure it. It has not been easy—far from it. During the past four and a half years, it has been my fate and my responsibility to be commander-in-chief. I have lived daily and nightly with the cost of this war. I know the pain that it has inflicted. I know perhaps better than anyone the misgivings that it has aroused.[10]

Throughout this entire, long period, I have been sustained by a single principle: that what we are doing now in Vietnam is vital not only to the security of Southeast Asia, but it is vital to the security of every American.

Surely we have treaties which we must respect. Surely we have commitments that we are going to keep. Resolutions of the Congress testify to the need to resist aggression in the world and in Southeast Asia. But the heart of our involvement in South Vietnam under three different Presidents, three separate administrations has always been America's own security. And the larger purpose of our involvement has always been to help the nations of Southeast Asia become independent and stand alone, self-sustaining as members of a great world community, at peace with themselves, and at peace with all others. With such an Asia, our country—and the world—will be far more secure than it is tonight.

I believe that a peaceful Asia is far nearer to reality because of what America has done in Vietnam. I believe that the men who endure the dangers of battle there, fighting there for us tonight, are helping the entire world avoid far greater conflicts, far wider wars, far more destruction, than this one.

[10] Why is the tone of this paragraph so much more emotional than the previous ones? How does it affect the speaker's credibility?

The peace that will bring them home some day will come. Tonight I have offered the first in what I hope will be a series of mutual moves toward peace. I pray that it will not be rejected by the leaders of North Vietnam. I pray that they will accept it as a means by which the sacrifices of their own people may be ended. And I ask your help and your support, my fellow citizens, for this effort to reach across the battlefield toward an early peace.[11]

Finally, my fellow Americans, let me say this: Of those to whom much is given, much is asked. I cannot say—and no man could say—that no more will be asked of us. Yet I believe that now, no less than when the decade began, this generation of Americans is willing to pay any price, bear any burden, meet any hardship, support any friend, oppose any foe, to assure the survival, and the success, of liberty.

Since those words were spoken by John F. Kennedy, the people of America have kept that compact with mankind's noblest cause. And we shall continue to keep it. Yet, I believe that we must always be mindful of this one thing, whatever the trials and the tests ahead. The ultimate strength of our country and our cause will lie, not in powerful weapons or infinite resources or boundless wealth, but will lie in the unity of our people. This I believe very deeply.[12]

Throughout my entire public career I have followed the personal philosophy that I am a free man, an American, a public servant and a member of my party—in that order—always and only. For thirty-seven years in the service of our nation, first as a Congressman, as a Senator and as Vice President, and now as your president, I have put the unity of the people first. I have put it ahead of any divisive partisanship. And in these times, as in times before, it is true that a house divided against itself by the spirit of faction, of party, of region, of religion, of race, is a house that cannot stand.

[11] This paragraph and the previous one are highly personalized. Delete "I believe," "I pray," and "I ask" and note the effect upon the strength of the arguments.

[12] Evaluate these statements as a transition and an introduction to the President's special announcement.

There is division in the American house now. There is divisiveness among us all tonight. And holding the trust that is mine, as president of all the people, I cannot disregard the peril to the progress of the American people and the hope and the prospect of peace for all peoples. So, I would ask all Americans, whatever their personal interests or concern, to guard against divisiveness and all its ugly consequences.[13]

Fifty-two months and ten days ago, in a moment of tragedy and trauma, the duties of this office fell upon me. I asked then for your help and God's, that we might continue America on its course binding up our wounds, healing our history, moving forward in new unity to clear the American agenda and to keep the American commitment for all of our people.

United we have kept that commitment. United we have enlarged that commitment. Through all time to come I think America will be a stronger nation, a more just society, a land of greater opportunity and fulfillment because of what we have all done together in these years of unparalleled achievement. Our reward will come in the life of freedom and peace and hope that our children will enjoy through ages ahead.

What we won when all of our people united just must not now be lost in suspicion, distrust, selfishness, and politics among any of our people. And believing this as I do, I have concluded that I should not permit the presidency to become involved in the partisan divisions that are developing in this political year.

With America's sons in the fields far away, with America's future under challenge right here at home, with our hopes and the world's hopes for peace in the balance every day, I do not believe that I should devote an hour or a day of my time to any personal partisan causes or to any duties other than the awesome duties of this office—the presidency of your country.

Accordingly, I shall not seek, and I will not accept, the nomination of my party for another term as your president.[14]

[13] What effect would the specific naming of his critics and denunciation of their tactics have had upon the quality of the speech?

[14] If this sentence had come at the beginning of this segment of the speech, what effect would it have had on audience interest and reaction?

But let men everywhere know, however, that a strong and a confident, and vigilant America stands ready tonight to seek an honorable peace; and stands ready tonight to defend an honored cause whatever the price, whatever the burden, whatever the sacrifices that duty may require. Thank you for listening. Good night and God bless all of you.

CRITICAL ANALYSIS AND PROJECTS

1. Johnson discussed three major topics in this address: a peace proposal, a tax bill, and his political future. How does he unify the speech?
2. Johnson has a fondness for "I believe," "I think," and similar first person usages. Delete as many as possible, or change the "I" to "we." Do the alterations make the language of the speech more forceful? Explain.
3. Is this speech primarily to inform or to persuade his listeners? How many audiences are there for this speech? How does the President appeal to each of them?
4. Would Johnson have strengthened his appeal for peace if he had announced his decision not to run for reelection at the beginning of his speech? What other strategies were available?
5. Prepare a speech in which you report the immediate critical reactions to this speech as they were reported in newspapers and magazines.
6. What effect will this speech have upon evaluations of Johnson as a president?
7. The Johnson administration has been criticized for failing to accept earlier peace overtures from Hanoi. Write an essay attacking or defending American attempts to negotiate a settlement in Vietnam.

SELECTED BIBLIOGRAPHY

1. Bell, Jack. *The Johnson Treatment*. New York: Harper and Row, 1965.
2. Broder, David S. "Great Speeches Aren't Necessarily Good Politics," *The New York Times Magazine* (March 29, 1964), pp. 7, 22, 24–25.
3. Cornwell, Elmer E., Jr. *Presidential Leadership of Public Opinion*. Bloomington, Ind.: Indiana University Press, 1965.

4. Eisner, Robert. "War and Taxes: The Role of the Economist in Politics," *Bulletin of the Atomic Scientists,* XXIV (June 1968), 13–18.
5. Gorden, William, and Robert Bunder. "The Sentimental Side of Mr. Johnson," *Southern Speech Journal,* XXXII (Fall 1966), 58–66.
6. Johnson, Lyndon B. *My Hope for America.* New York: Random House, 1964.
7. ———. *A Time for Action: A Selection from the Speeches and Writings of Lyndon B. Johnson, 1953–1964.* New York: Atheneum Publishers, 1964.
8. McNamara, Robert S. *The Essence of Security: Reflections in Office,* ed. Henry Trewhitt. New York: Harper and Row, 1968.
9. Phelps, Waldo, and Andrea Beck. "Lyndon Johnson's Address at the U.C.L.A. Charter Day Ceremony," *Western Speech,* XXIX (Summer 1965), 162–171.
10. Provence, Harry. *Lyndon B. Johnson: A Biography.* New York: Fleet Publishing Corporation, 1964.
11. Roberts, Charles. *LBJ's Inner Circle.* New York: Delacorte Press, 1965.
12. White, Theodore H. *The Making of the President, 1964.* New York: Atheneum Publishers, 1965.

A NOTE ON THE TYPE

This book was set on the Linotype in Baskerville. The punches for this face were cut under the supervision of George W. Jones, the eminent English printer and the designer of Granjon and Estienne. Linotype Baskerville is a facsimile cutting from type cast from the original matrices of a face designed by John Baskerville, a writing master of Birmingham, for his own private press. The original face was the forerunner of the "modern" group of type faces, known today as Scotch, Bodoni, etc. After his death in 1775, Baskerville's punches and matrices were sold in France and were used to produce the sumptuous Kehl edition of Voltaire's works.

This book was composed, printed and bound by H. Wolff Book Manufacturing Co., Inc., New York, N.Y.

Typography by Antonia Krass